John Gittus is a well-seasoned self-made businessman, who attributes many of his advantages in life to his acquired skills in negotiation… He is a great believer in experiencing every step for himself before moving on in business to the next challenge. Only then he says can you write with authority and help others to reach similar levels of success. From his early beginnings he progressed to key positions in industry and commerce and worked alongside heads of international public limited companies and others in the public domain throughout his career. He is married with two grown up children, an endurance athlete with a keen interest in sport and political affairs, and an avid world traveller and adventurer.

To Judy and Colin,
with all my love,

It would be my hope that this timeless work may endure for my future
generations engaged in the exhilarating activity we call negotiating.

# John Gittus

# Negotiation

"A Management Tool"

AUSTIN MACAULEY PUBLISHERS™

LONDON · CAMBRIDGE · NEW YORK · SHARJAH

A CIP catalogue record for this title is available from the British Library.

ISBN 9781398457119 (Paperback)
ISBN 9781398457126 (ePub e-book)

www.austinmacauley.com

First Published 2022
Austin Macauley Publishers Ltd
1 Canada Square
Canary Wharf
London
E14 5AA

# Table of Contents

Chapter 1 Preface                                            10

Chapter 2 Introduction                                       19

Chapter 3 The Basics                                         24

Chapter 4 Tactical Ploys                                     34

Chapter 5 Haggling                                           46

Chapter 6 The Wedding                                        52

Chapter 7 Your Rights                                        56

Chapter 8 Selling an Asset                                   66

Chapter 9 Sundry Cases                                       70

Chapter 10 On a Lighter Note                                 75

Chapter 11 The Shake-Up                                      82

Chapter 12 Roadblocks                                        86

Chapter 13 In the High Court                                 89

Chapter 14 The Chat in the Urinals                           98

Chapter 15 The Russian Job                                  105

Chapter 16 Negotiating with Banks                           108

Chapter 17 Consolidating Rights                             114

Chapter 18 The Way Out                                      119

Chapter 19 On Opening a Railway Station                     126

Chapter 20 Zimbabwe                                         132

**Chapter 21 Trading Blocks and Cartels**     139

**Chapter 22 Travelling Here and Beyond**     142

**Chapter 23 Dangerous Liaisons**     146

**Chapter 24 Joining a Stock Market**     156

**Chapter 25 The Management Buy-Out**     160

**Chapter 26 At the Royal Court**     174

**Chapter 27 Dealing with Demigods**     179

**Chapter 28 The Hit Squad**     185

**Chapter 29 In the Written Form**     190

**Chapter 30 The Wooden Spoon**     214

**Chapter 31 Conclusion**     217

*Watton-at-Stone station, Hertfordshire, the first to be opened in modern times after successful negotiations led by the author.*

# Chapter 1
# Preface

Before writing this book, it seemed reasonable that I should justify what experience I have in the subject.

These pages map out the route taken from my early beginnings to the days when negotiation became the greatest strength of my career. It is a vast subject, and real expertise in its application is built up over time. Many don't seriously negotiate at all but seek the easiest route to agreement when they could do so very much better. And it is only by experiencing the treatment of a whole range of negotiating skills that this becomes fully apparent. The route taken from my early days into my career and beyond will illuminate how the subject played such an important and effective role in my success. There is no greater or enduring asset that influenced my progress quite so much. I strongly recommend it to all budding and experienced businessmen and women and others, both in their personal and their business lives.

Netley Abbey just a few miles along the coast from Southampton, next before the better-known yachting centre of Hamble-le-Rice was a sleepy little village. It had the ruins of an abbey built by the Cistercian monks in the early thirteenth century, a castle used as a rest home for the elderly, two pubs, a small cinema closed long since, a tiny infant school, post office, fish and chip shop, a farm on the fringe of the village, and little else. On the outskirts stood the Royal Victoria Hospital, at one time the longest such building in the world, built in an Indian style to please Queen Victoria herself. It served as a respite for soldiers shipped home from the war with mental damage. It was during the war that I lived in Netley with my mother, courtesy of my grandparents, whilst my father fought in the war. People were more stationary in those days so I was surrounded by relatives, save for those lost in battle. The enemy frequently targeted the docks and a strategic railway line running at the end of our road which carried troops on manoeuvres.

The drone of enemy planes day or night would see us rush down to our Anderson shelter. During the day I would be fascinated by the sight of ships entering and leaving the Southampton water and wondered where they might be going and whether I might even travel on them one day.

Queen Victoria arrived at the hard near the hospital one day by boat from her home at Osborne House on the Isle of Wight. As usual on such occasions she was met by a line of mothers showing off their babies. When the queen asked my great grandmother to reveal her baby, she pulled the covers back, only for the queen to denounce her as an ugly baby and demand she be covered up "at once!" Gran became anti-royalist and left wing instantly, even though she opened two businesses when widowed at the age of forty-five, having sworn never to take a penny from the state. She started a laundry business for officers only, but one day during a dock strike had to row out to the ships herself to collect the laundry when her staff refused to take on the risk. She was eighty-five at the time!

I'm certain that the driving forces shaping your career are much influenced by your early experiences. As young as I was, I would often sit on the corner of the street contemplating my future. That I was surrounded by a rather unconventional mix of people didn't offer much inspiration to draw upon! My gran had retired by the time I might have been influenced by her example, and otherwise there was little else to encourage my early thoughts. My aunt worked on the production of parts for the spitfire, and an uncle fired millions of rivets into newly built ships for fifty years. He was never late for work, never ill and never joined any strikes, and this diligence over such a long time earned him the OBE – that is to say simply for being a well-regarded employee!

An older uncle was partially mentally impaired after cracking his head as he tripped into the Anderson shelter. A popular uncle would stroll down the road shaking a few coins in his pocket boasting "one day I'll be rich my boy; you'll see!" which was as likely to happen as men arriving from Mars. So not much of an influence there! His teenage son could have played the part of the spiv in Dad's Army. According to him we were the last line of defence against the enemy. He had us picking up sticks and stones in readiness to defend our sisters and mothers! And my carefully chosen stone remained ever ready in my pocket until the very last shots of war. Only on VE day did I allow it to trickle through my fingers onto the ground! A woman living along the road would lean on her gate post and ask every passer-by if they were "putting it about she was barmy!" My grandmother was my favourite and my grandfather was a kindly old man, and a proud member of the Home Guard. He would push me along to his allotment in his wheelbarrow to "dig for victory" and I would entertain him with my chatter.

That is until the day an enemy plane flew directly over in the direction of our home with the obvious aim of bombing the strategic railway line. My grandfather in rage shook his fist at him, a thinly veiled attempt at negotiating a better outcome that was bound to fail, but then the plane was flying directly towards his house! The pilot spotted the gesture, and turned full circle to empty his machine guns on us. At my grandfather's instigation we got down fast and he lay over me for protection, quite prepared to sacrifice his own life for me. Once the pilot had turned and continued on his way, we recovered only to find what I referred to as "those angry holes!" They ran the entire length of my body and less than half an inch away, singing my shorts at one point! Smoke and soil fragments were still rising from each of them. Without my grandfather's quick thinking I wouldn't be writing this book today! Realising his mistake, and fearful he would get the blame, I was sworn to secrecy and I kept that secret until long after his death, and very nearly my mother's also. Such a lesson in confidentially goes hand in hand with taking responsibility in industry, in negotiating and in general, and it was never lost on me. The war ended and the reunited family moved to the Midlands to be close to industry for my father's work, but six years of war cost him his career and very nearly his life, and I suppose mine also remembering that day down the allotments.

As it was times were very hard and there was always friction over money, even after the years of rationing.

These were the early experiences that influenced my entry into the world of business where I would in the course of time engage with aristocrats and giants of industry. You had to be tough in those days, also determined but essentially optimistic. My own experiences made me very much aware of scarcity and the prime need for security. At that time, I neither had the resources nor the inclination to be an entrepreneur although I greatly admired others who were. Instead, as I entered work, I decided to focus on acquiring the skills and attributes that would be of value to industrialists. Over time, as I sharpened my negotiation skills, I realised just how highly they featured in everything I accomplished.

Sitting on that corner of the street contemplating my future I knew that being a train driver or fireman and suchlike never appealed to me for a moment. I knew then that "things happened" in companies. Products were made and sold, and this required management of some kind, and organisation. That was to be my direction of travel and I had an inkling of it even then.

It was when I was around nine or ten, I got my first shot at negotiating. As young boys we used to exchange comics, and I had a particular bent at getting more back than I gave out. Firstly, if I had already read an issue on offer but had a rarer American copy to hand, I would ask for two-for-one. And then when the American one was offered back to me, I would argue I had already read it, so it lost its value and I would exchange on a one-for-one basis! Another line of negotiation was to argue one thick comic justified an exchange for two thinner ones, and so on. In time a line of mothers arrived at our door protesting that I now held every comic in the road. None of their sons had a single comic to their name! I argued it was "free enterprise" but needless to say I was compelled to redistribute them all. But the lesson had been leaned, and furthermore it had been fun!

Of working age, I joined a major clearing bank, but that offered nothing to test you until you reached the ranks of manager, and the incumbent manager was such a snob I think he sensed my dislike of him. The junior staff seemed to be in complete ignorance as to exactly what happened in industry. It was as though they deduced that those having a high overdraft must be non-disciplined renegades it was our ill fortune to serve! The manager and I fell out badly when I stood in the middle of his highly polished floor dripping mud. I had already committed one offence when I wheeled my newly acquired bicycle through the hall to show my friends, but worse was to come. Right at the end of a soccer match in which I had just scored the referee blew his whistle, to be followed more or less instantly by the whistle indicating the end of the game. Then a different kind of whistle could be heard from more than one direction as several policemen invaded the pitch heading in my direction! Perhaps they supported the other side and were angry I had scored, but I was bundled into a police car and driven to the branch right in the very centre of town. On arrival I heard a thousand raised voices, and as I got out of the car, still in full soccer regalia, a gasp went up from the gathering crowd. No doubt they thought I had been apprehended as the "inside man" in the assumed bank robbery that was taking place. Dripping mud, and carrying the match ball over my back, I was led into the bank where I was asked to take an armed officer down to the vaults. As it happened nothing had been disturbed and it all turned out to be a false alarm. It only occurred to me afterwards that it was because I was a named key holder rather than a suspect I had been "arrested" without explanation. The unwillingness of the police to tell me what was going on merely raised my fears as to their intentions. What was worse was that I inevitably dripped mud onto the manager's precious banking floor, and when he arrived twenty minutes after me to be confronted by an ever-growing crowd he was less than pleased. That I was there ahead of him dripping mud did nothing to advance my career which was soon to be placed in serious jeopardy and ended prematurely! So my career in banking was short lived, but I had the satisfaction of knowing the manager was subsequently castigated by an inspection team for having lost me. We didn't have the advantage in those far off days of ultra-efficient computers so much of the recording was done by hand using basic adding machines. It fell to me to "balance the day's work" as we called it before staff could go home. The manager had to employ several people, I was informed, to cover my workload and nobody got home early ever again! When the manager offered me my old job back there are no prizes for guessing my reaction!

This turned out to be the greatest blessing in disguise. The job was nothing more than "number crunching," and the thought that junior staff would get anywhere near a negotiating situation would have been laughable. All it taught me was that the manager attracted new customers on the golf course on a Sunday. Any new customer was passed on to a "negotiation circle" or cartel wherein his insurance friends insured the customer, and his solicitor friends covered his legal requirements. Those who first met one of the other two pillars of the "club" were duly passed on to the others in like manner.

In contrast my first experience in industry in a structural steel engineering and stockholding company gave me valuable insight into how industry worked. I had lost the so-called security of the bank, but the door was finally open to discover the way into industrial management. I knew that accountancy would provide me the optimum route since that discipline was ideally placed, and from its sources came many of the most successful industrial managers. But I couldn't afford that at the time, and in any case, it would have to wait until after my much-deferred national service. By then Chartered Accountants firms for the first time paid you a modest salary whilst you were being trained. I had regretted turning down what would have been the very last national service commission ever offered, but instead was elevated to the War Office. There I gained valuable insights into the thinking and procedures of the Civil Service, and served my country well by catching a Russian spy red handed. On my demob a gathering of over a hundred officers turned the tables and saluted me as being representative of the last conscripts who had served the Army over the years. I returned the salute and returned to "civvy street" as we called it to resume my much-delayed career. That was the consequence of having to wait three years before the last conscripts were trickle fed into the regular army, and then serving two years plus a further six months tagged onto the end. At the age of twenty-three, my career had hardly started.

In an effort to determine my future I took a solo cycle ride to Italy during which I resolved I would decide whether or not I would make further sacrifices and embark on qualifying, or leave my career to waste. I returned refreshed having decided it would be a travesty to abandon my career so I would make the sacrifice and get on with the job in hand. And it was the example of my army experience itself that gave me the means of doing so. My reasoning was that if the army could, by one means or another, cause you to perfect some twenty-seven rifle and drill movements in a matter of weeks then I would apply the same vigour to qualifying. I joined a very old-fashioned firm of Chartered Accountants, Scattergood Drinkwater and Sons, and had dealings with a great many small, medium sized, and larger firms whilst I was learning the trade. I was fully qualified within three years as opposed to the normal expectation of five or six years, and you could say the catalyst for this was the "negotiation" I held with myself en route to San Remo.

Now my journey was about to commence in earnest. Firstly, the Dunlop rubber company, then the machine tool industry, the construction industry and next the commercial catering equipment industry. In my thirst for knowledge and skills I only every remained long enough to feel I had taken in all there was to learn, and then I moved on improving my lot at the same time. At the age of twenty-nine I finally felt I had caught up with my peers when I was for the first time promoted to the board of directors, and was participating in high level negotiations and administrative responsibilities as I had always intended.

By then I was sitting alongside very successful industrialists such as Sir Ian Morrow and others. Ian had been part of the team that went out to the United States as a young man negotiating the Marshall Aid Plan after the war. He was President of the Scottish Institute of Chartered Accountants, founded the consultants Robson Morrow, and took on literally hundreds of directorships in industry. He became deputy chairman of Hambros Bank, was appointed by the government to "rescue" the Rolls Royce aero engine company, and subsequently to lead an investigation into Lloyds stockbrokers, and much more besides. He was regarded as the first "company doctor" being called in frequently to rescue one firm or another. But he never left our company, and I had a very close association with him for sixteen years. Ian mixed with Presidents of the US and many others of distinction, whilst my local managing director was enormously proud of his invitations to dine with royalty, having been awarded the Royal Warrant.

Ronnie Hooker was the President of the institute of mechanical engineers and also held the same post for the body of electrical engineers. He also had numerous directorships throughout industry. And when I got promoted up to the main board my chairman was D'Arcy Biss who also chaired the board of Cunard, the Ritz hotel and numerous others. He was a renowned Oxford scholar who headed up a major firm of solicitors in the city from whom I also gained much knowledge on a multitude of matters of relevance to industrialists. On the same board was Barrie Stephens who built up the massive Siebe organisation and became a billionaire in the process. We had the chairman of Reeds, the two Wiseman brothers brought up in the spectacle industry, a patent expert and a representative from the contact lens industry all sitting on our board.

I was engaged in business with a great many distinguished people yet only two of us had been so elevated whilst being a generation younger. You can't sit alongside such people day by day without being exposed to, and taking part in major negotiations. A huge number of ideas, tips, reactions to situations, firefighting emergencies and so on came to my regular notice and involvement. Most of the directors on the main board were non-executive and I carried a major share of conducting negotiations myself. The ethos and atmosphere in which we conducted our business served as a massive inspiration. The more senior members were in the main what we would today regard as billionaires, and independent as such, whereas my livelihood rested wholly on my day-to-day performance.

The experiences of the lessons learned led to my writing my first book entitled Croner's Guide to Cost Control published back in 1974. By now I was also coming to the realisation I had never come across a book on the subject of negotiation, and that there was currently a huge gap to fill. With a good number of successful negotiations behind me I spoke to Croner who welcomed the idea of publishing such a work, so I commenced writing it during my leisure time. However, it was my promotion to our main board and other pressures that meant I couldn't complete it in good time. Instead, I heard from my go-between that they were "having a go" at writing the book themselves. Soon "negotiation" became the catch word throughout industry. Books came from all directions, seminars, consultations and almost an entire industry it seemed was fully established. But I had missed the boat!

Right then I learned one of the most valuable lessons in negotiation, that is to say to keep your cards close to your chest until an appropriate time to reveal them! So, you may well ask what inspires me to write such a book now, well into my retirement, and all these many years later. The simple answer is that the rest of my career added enormously to my first-hand experiences and my authority on the subject. Until now I never had the opportunity, but the urge never left me.

My appointment to my first main board was with an international plc, the major manufacturer of its product in the world. I never forgot my curiosity driven by the shipping along the Southampton water, but my responsibilities had never taken me out of Europe. That is to say until Mugabe took over in a vicious civil war in Africa when my company "volunteered" me to go down there to discover if our subsidiary still existed! I had finally been allowed out of my backyard and now I travelled the world on business and for pleasure, not stopping until I had visited every country bar two that existed at the time of my birth. There is no greater means of acquiring experience than through travel which of itself exposes you to all the vagaries, complications and customs worldwide, and places you in multiple negotiating positions to sharpen your skills.

Then followed a spell helping a company in heavy engineering to launch onto the now defunct Unlisted Securities Market. I was offered a position on the main board of Scottish and Newcastle breweries, a top thirty company, by David Balfour, chairman as he was also of the Chartered Bank. This was followed by a management buyout of a group at the retail end of spectacles, for which I was made chairman and chief executive. And finally, a spell in the motor industry before reaching my ultimate goal of retiring at the age of fifty.

The driving forces behind my career are easy to see. They started with the need to simply survive, to gain security, and only then the search for job fulfilment and my contribution to industry was realised. I learned how to fight from my corner, how to show determination and how negotiation skills were of vital concern central to everything I ever achieved. I negotiated my way out of hugely dangerous situations and overcame hurdles few can have experienced. I recognised the importance of respecting confidentiality and of taking responsibility.

With so much more negotiating experience, I now feel better qualified by far than I was in those earlier days, and this book has been in my head waiting to be written for a very long time. I feel it represents a different kind of work to most because it is more than a hard dry read of theory, combining as it does a large number of real-life anecdotes which reiterate the principles whilst still retaining interest and hopefully entertainment value. It is not based on the premise that I have anything new to teach experienced businessmen and women, rather as a means of refreshing skills they will in the main already possess. I hope this work will perhaps encourage them to take a fresh look at the subject, to remind them of those skills, perhaps enhance new skills, and to kindle renewed interest. It has been a long time coming but finally arrived, and I very much hope it will prove of value and of interest to my readers.

# Chapter 2
# Introduction

In its broadest sense negotiation is ever present. It invades every walk of life, even if you are not conscious of it, both in business and our private lives. When people think of negotiation, they generally think of a number of well-suited men sat in a board room hammering out a deal with other equally equipped executives. But that approach denies ordinary folk from recognising and taking advantage of their negotiating skills. For committed executives they are sold short because they are not fully aware of the opportunities that arise in all situations throughout the day. So, the subject is much wider than commonly thought and it will be my intention to approach the subject from many angles.

A negotiation does not start when a number of persons meet in that board room. Negotiations commence almost without you being conscious of the fact, and usually some time before you get down to sitting around a table to discuss a proposition in earnest. Every negotiation has to have a starting point, and once this is triggered you can say you are in full negotiation mode. And trigger points can be immensely varied. Actions substitute for verbal negotiations in a great many instances. A simple nod might be intended as an invitation to negotiate, and some actions or other utterances may be regarded as tacit negotiations in their own right. A proposal to open discussions on any matter involving mixed interests is a negotiation.. It might be in the full business sense or it might, for example, simply be between man and wife. A promise to do something on condition that somebody else takes a certain action is a negotiation in itself, concluded when the other person acquiesces. It starts when you ask for a commitment and is completed when agreement is reached. In business negotiations are commonly far more complex but this is not necessarily so even there. Very often more might have been made of them but one or other party has missed the opportunity. Negotiation involves the use of a whole range of approaches and tactics that form almost a language in its own right. All these variations are what you may regard as branches of the extensive art of negotiation, and they will be fully addressed. This will be by analysis of their characteristics as such and in the anecdotal case studies that follow. These are drawn from my own experiences over a long career. By the time you complete the reading of this work you should have added something to your comprehensive knowledge of this intriguing subject.

As a general rule nothing gets done without negotiation, or at least nothing gets done well. If you just accept conditions thrust upon you then you will always be at the losing end of the bargain. And for the same reason you should not rush to an agreement without fully exploiting all the techniques at your disposal. Firstly, you should familiarise yourself with the facts and your objectives, and then use your acquired techniques to obtain the best deal. Negotiation should never be seen as just a burden but that which takes you into a world of dynamic enterprise rather than the inertia of standing still. It opens up possibilities you may never have dreamed of. It has taken me into the company of giants of industry and commerce, with officials of the European Union at Brussels, and out of the most tricky personal dilemmas, and much besides. It can be career enhancing by alerting your employers to your accomplishments, an essential asset if you intend to progress in business.

In our private lives negotiation is also ever present. Making a date is a negotiation. If you set up home with your partner, then it continues for as long as you are together. How to furnish a room, where to go on holiday, and so on in their simplest form are negotiations, and all men know that a bunch of flowers for their wives is a very sound opening gambit! Over time you realise you are subtly applying well-trodden paths and tested techniques, and this book would be incomplete if we did not give some hints herein on that very wide field of interest. The objective of this work is to help you adopt a methodical and prepared approach to matters that are of the greatest significance to us all. This is so whether you are engaged in significant business situations such as producing and selling a product, building an airport, providing consumables to the market, meeting challenges in day-to-day life and a zillion other things.

The format of a negotiation is almost as important as its substance. One assumes there must as a minimum be one party on each side of the discussion, but there may be a substantial number on both sides or very often just one person facing a greater number. Both sides have to be satisfied before anything can be concluded, and in the absence of agreement you should not flog a dead horse. Just part company with your position and honour intact.

In trade there is a well-tried path which commences with a party seeking business from some quarter or other, perhaps responding to an advert or approaching known suppliers, conducting negotiations, arriving at an agreed offer and acceptance, and finally proceeding to contract and completion. And this may of course be for a product or a service of one kind or another. This will usually involve giving the agreed contract legal effect, either by exchange of letters or in a formally drafted legal document. In the case of international matters, a Treaty. And as an interim stage these complex negotiations can pro temps be witnessed by way of a "Heads of Agreement" summary. This will serve as a record of the issues agreed to that point so that further negotiations can resume from that starting position. It may be used when there is far too much involved to sit through massive transactions such as the building of the third runway at Heathrow in one go, or if progress has to be halted temporarily whilst further investigations or preparatory steps are first concluded. All these steps are stages towards the final goal. Negotiating is thus a vital part of the chain of business activity itself. It is inherent in any kind of business and has been since the beginning of mankind.

The subject can be under-valued. There seems to be an ingrained acceptance that negotiation just means you bat the subject around for a while and then reach that famous "British compromise." This is a highly inadequate defeatist way of thinking. It leads to a practice of fixing your terms or your price artificially high so that when a compromise is struck you remain happy with the outcome. But that misses everything that negotiation in the true sense is about, and you will never optimise the result through that simplistic approach! If it has a role anywhere it would be in simple haggling techniques, but even that sells them short as you will see in a later chapter. Such an approach is completely devoid of technique, and if you depend upon it as your basic method, you are missing the main chance over and over again.

At a personal level each party puts the other on trust that he or she will not renegue on what has been agreed. If either party does then they lose faith, and this will rebound against them in the future. So, when we negotiate the consequence of our actions assumes great importance, both short term and long term. With trust comes the expectation that each party is being honest and fully transparent. But we all know that in the cut and thrust of business this is more often far from the case.

The legal system in our country is far advanced and plays an essential role in the chain of events once a negotiated agreement is reached. But if the legal contract does not exactly mirror what has been agreed you are in trouble at the outset. Never trust that in drafting the contract your solicitors or legal department have properly reflected your instructions. The entire benefit of what has been negotiated can be thrown away at this point without you even noticing it! It is quite common for many executives, flushed with excitement at their most recent conquest, to rush off immediately for the next. They leave somebody else inadequately prepared to deal with the paperwork. In my experience this is the most common area of disaster!

The world of business and commerce is of course intensely competitive, some describing it as a "rat race," so if you want to survive and prosper tools such as good negotiating skills are essential. They are well worth the time spent familiarising yourself with them. The following chapters will illustrate key negotiating principles and ploys throughout, either through a systematic explanation of the theory or as promised subsequently through the case studies drawn from my own experience. As you read through these cases you will spot for yourself when one or other principle or tactic has been employed. By the end it is hoped you will have been stimulated such that your thinking in any situation is all the sharper, and that you will be better equipped to meet the challenges of your next enterprise. It is hoped that by the time you have completed your reading of this work your skills will be fully refreshed and the language second nature.

The case studies chosen lay all the facts bare, and nothing has been glossed over. They are all real and none are imagined. No attempt has been made to exaggerate or hide them, win or lose. Errors and flaws, successes and failures are included alike as what better way to heed them and learn. It is intended to be instructive. No criticism is made or implied to any character, disclosed or otherwise. It must be noted that all the executives and others I have had dealings with have, like myself, been engaged in the honest pursuit of trade and business, save where personal events may arise. If I regard any of them in any particular light, I am doing so to highlight the background to particular events, and nothing further. As with my readers we are all contributing massively to the economy and our capitalist system to the best of our ability, and our collective skills are indeed the reason why our country is acknowledged as one of the most successful in the world.

A number of cases outline what was found to be the best means of extracting myself from situations in which my very life was at stake. The examples show how you can quickly develop the right mood in which to survive, both from what you do and say and more so what you refrain from doing and saying. It has been my experience it seems to run into a rather large number of such instances, and I have little doubt that the combination of native wit and negotiating skills has seen me survive over the years when I might not have done so. It is something from which we can all learn to our advantage.

# Chapter 3
# The Basics

Before we study real life illustrations, we should first obtain a basic understanding of negotiating principles.

Values

Whether it is for a business seeking to enhance its profits or an individual or organisation wishing to maximise value it is assumed in all cases that we are looking for the best outcome commensurate with commitment. Value is more than just obtaining the lowest price and can be judged by a number of considerations, for example:

Quality – will it be of sound construction and reliable?

Delivery – when will I get it?

After service – what happens if it goes wrong?

Guarantee – for what period and on what terms is it guaranteed?

Exclusivity – will I gain exclusivity for the product or service?

Price protection – for how long and on what terms will each party to the transaction be locked in?

Discounts – how can these be maximised and are further quantity discounts built in?

There will of course be a great many more which will be most apparent to the parties familiar with the transaction.

## The incremental Pathway to Success

A business is only ever as good as the sum of its parts, and one can think of these as the accumulation of countless transactions already made, those yet to be negotiated, ongoing contracts, efficiency enhancing capital investments and the skills of its management team through experience, knowledge, determination and enterprise. Each and every one of these is the result of individual improvements over time in each area. This is particularly so in the investment choices made and through the outcome of successful negotiations. Each transaction adds marginal value to the whole so if the trend is to constantly add good marginal value per transaction, then the overall result will be ever upwards to success, and the opposite applies with equal measure. And if we acknowledge that no transaction on Earth can be concluded in the absence of negotiation, then you will quickly acknowledge the essential importance of negotiation skills in maximising individual and accumulative results of any business.

Ask yourself, could you have done better in your last negotiation? If the answer is "yes" then the deal you accepted will have to that extent watered down your overall success. It is usually then too late to do much about it. If the answer is "no" then prospectively you are working towards success, and will continue to do so as long as you maximise all such transactions. Ask yourself if you have this "incremental brain set" approach as I call it? If not, then consider the advantages of cultivating such a manner of thinking both for yourself and throughout your organisation.

## Return on Capital Employed

We measure individual well-being and satisfaction by many values, and negotiation plays a pivotal role in enhancing prosperity. Business success in financial terms is usually measured by the level of profits, but this is rather meaningless in the true sense of the word if it is not related to the size of the company, the physical assets and the total capital employed in it long term. In other words, the not quite so oft used term, return on capital employed. If we think of capital employed itself as the sum of past investment choices over time it will readily be accepted that the selection of these, and the terms upon which they are accepted will likewise determine the overall performance. As we weed out non-profitable investments, avoid making future mistakes, and inject ever better investments the incremental impact of these will restore and enhance the overall result. And right at the core of this process is good judgement and sound negotiation in acquiring the means by which we meet our goals.

## Our Goals

Having determined what is of value to us we need to know what our goals are or we will be floundering around in the dark! Goals are carried in the head by some folk, but the more methodical amongst us will develop a written business plan with all the vagaries and assumptions built into it and specified as such. This affords you the chance to identify shortcomings, and to offset them with remedial action if your operation strays off course. To meet our goals, we will develop our best strategic path forward, then consider which tactics may be employed to achieve them. Given the wealth of literature on both strategic planning and business tactics I do not propose to dwell on these important facets but will remain focused on the employment and role of negotiating in the overall process.

## The Venue

It is relevant to consider where negotiating takes place and what might serve us best, but we should remember that not all negotiating by any means is done with a team around a boardroom. Very often, perhaps in the majority of cases it is done on a one-to-one basis, and the venue can be the board room, a pub or a chance meeting on public transport to name but a few. In such a case you need to have your wits about you and your skills sharpened as such meetings are usually quite unexpected, and you will not want to be caught wanting. Negotiating instantly or "on the hoof" as you might say can be very exhilarating and rewarding for the better prepared, but a nightmare for those that are not!

In deciding the venue to hold the meeting you may prefer your premises where you can show your product or service off to your best ability. You may have very good reasons to keep strangers off your premises for fear of giving away confidential information. Not many give much thought to the role the chosen venue may have of itself on the outcome so it is worth considering.

## Composition of the Team

To avoid confusion and conflict in the meeting it is essential you determine in advance who is going to take the senior or more experienced role and head up the team. Sometimes members of teams can contradict each other and throw a spanner in the works just when you are making progress. So for myself I prefer to conduct negotiations on a one-to-one basis unless I need to call on experts in particular areas or feel that the weight of numbers would be of advantage to me. And when you do negotiate on a one-to-one basis you can usually be that more confident that your opposite number has the authority to make any decisions. A team of negotiators descending on you I have found is more likely to herald the fact they have to refer the final decision "upstairs" as we say.

When it comes to team selection it goes without saying you may need to call on the special talents of marketing personnel, the technical knowledge of engineers or research and development personnel and so on. Even previously satisfied customers are sometimes willing to speak for you if you have a good relationship with them, the more so if they might gain something in the process. Or you may wish to conceal vital technical knowledge in which case you may not want to risk having such an expert anywhere on hand for fear of disclosure. Nor will you want to conduct a tour of that part of your factory or organisation where sensitive information can be viewed. And we most certainly don't want to do a "Joseph," being my pet name for a faux pas on such an occasion you will encounter later.

## Preparing for a Formal Negotiation

In preparing for a formal meeting, it is an essential prerequisite you and your team determine in advance what it is you seek to achieve, what are your aims, what have you to offer, what you think or may glean your opposite number has to offer, what price you are prepared to pay, or value you may be prepared to surrender and in what circumstances you would walk away abandoning further discussion. You should know each and every detail of every aspect of the situation you can collect together before taking any further steps.

There is no unwritten rule that says parties must come to an agreement. Negotiations are often purely exploratory to see if there is anything worth taking further. In either case both parties can leave as good friends to do business another day. And when I say "both" parties bear in mind that in more complex cases more than two parties are commonly involved. Look no further than the third runway at Heathrow airport again to realise just how many parties are involved there. My first responsibility upon appointment to the main board was to join experts from numerous organisations around a huge boardroom table to set up a rights issue of shares in the City. It was rather like an action committee in the main, but a good example of the commitments being made by anything up to thirty persons around that single table, each representing a negotiated action path party by party.

In general, knowing the determining factors of your position in advance is of paramount importance. And bear in mind there is always a danger, once involved in negotiations the thrill and excitement of it all can very often drive you on to the wrong outcome. It can be as though the negotiations carry their own impetus in their own right. Pride may be at stake. Somebody's pet project or "sacred cow" may wrongly influence the result, or that may arise out of pure misguided recklessness. In such a case you will surely regret the outcome, perhaps for a very long time. Always remember that negotiating is not an end in itself!

### Early Motivators

As alluded to negotiations commence as a rule long before you have recognized they have. Odd comments or gestures set the mood, and accompanying hints lead you into full blown meaningful negotiations in direct result. Even as early as this in the negotiating process it is important to rebut any comments that place your opposite number on higher ground once you negotiate in earnest. Be quick thinking and sharp enough to counter any points you may feel are scored against you. These mood setting actions and comments do count if you don't deal with them at source. You will do well to recognise when you are being invited to negotiate since, from the odd remark or gesture, it is not always apparently obvious. Native wit has a very important role to play in the negotiating process, probably every bit as important as all the well-rehearsed tactics you will have in your armoury with the experiences you meet along the way.

### The Initial Stage of the Meeting

At all costs commence the meeting in a sense of well-being showing genuine concern for the interests of the opposite party. This will always serve your interests best. A cordial atmosphere will, of itself, smooth your way to a potentially successful outcome. And note well that a sense of humour is worth gold. In showing empathy and understanding for the other's wants you build his confidence, and he is more likely to return the gesture. If you can demonstrate you are willing to help him in his particular aims your success will be all the greater. The relationship may last for years and the transaction on the table may be the first of many. You will most usually want to make and preserve friendships. Antagonise people at your peril! Be prepared to be flexible if you can as this will only help your own cause. In negotiations some flexibility is always anticipated, and if you show none you will not get very far.

Know at the commencement what you regard as "not negotiable" at any price. And when you say something is not negotiable do so without any sign of doubt reflecting in your face, or in your voice. If you mean it when you speak it your opposite number will more likely accept it on face value. Remember that that little phrase is one of the most powerful and effective in your whole negotiating armoury!

## Negotiations in Earnest

With everybody at ease one party will open up the discussion, most commonly either the hosts or the party who has something to offer. People are not usually tongue tied at this point and conversation should flow quite naturally. You may feel your position is better served letting the other side make the running whilst you absorb what they have to say, or you may want to set the scene yourself and more especially if you want to emphasise some "red line" or precondition before proceeding further.

You may want to get any awkward "confessions" off your chest up-front at the outset. By this means the matter at hand is taken more lightly than would be the case if your guests should winkle them out, or they are revealed at a later stage. And you will always be in a much stronger position if you seek out possible obstacles in advance and establish your position towards them with your team.

As the discussions continue both sides will hold it in their interests to deduce what is important to their opposite number, what is not being revealed, where relative weaknesses lie, and above all who has the authority to decide. Who is most likely to give more ground than the others or can be prompted to be more honest than the others? Who will most likely give valuable points away!? If you think you know the answer to these questions then exploit them all you can but without making your ploy too obvious.

I remember once negotiating with a Jim Alsdorf of the Alsdorf Corporation in the US. When he heard our arguments and what we were seeking he simply said in a broad American accent, "Well you see, I just don't want to give away any points!" Well, neither did we, but how do you respond to such a naively

29

simple assertion!? Jim was extremely well off with his own art gallery containing paintings from some of the most famous artists in the world so he was not so much in need. Getting him to concede anything was like trying to get blood out of a stone. His beautiful young wife he brought along was very disarming, and it seemed to me that was the entire reason for her presence, so there's a tip for you!

Outside of walking away we didn't have much to counter with, but the fact our managing director had met him the night before and told him not to be offended by our approach didn't do much to enhance our chances. Our entire negotiating position had been compromised before we started! Neither did our managing director attend to rebalance the situation! That our party consisted of two or three members didn't help on this occasion because, having walked into such a situation scope for discussion amongst ourselves was compromised, and nobody took the lead to express how indignant or aggrieved we felt by Jim's stance. Had just one of our number been present that member could have taken the decision into his own hands if he were brave enough to do so! All we could do was threaten to abandon the product line but that was never going to happen. Nevertheless, as a negotiation principle "taking umbrage" can be a very powerful weapon in its right place which should be noted.

### Spotting the Weakest Link

Knowing which of the opposite team is their weakest link can be very useful. If you want a reaction to a point-blank question he is as likely as any to fluster and give away more than his colleagues may wish. Or he may attempt to cover his nerves by being more forthcoming with minimal prompting. Remain silent for a few moments and such persons often cover their discomfort by giving away far more than might be wise! So the question arises how would you spot such an individual other than having a degree in mind reading?

It never fails to surprise me is just how much you can read from a person's demeanour and their actions. Under pressure people give away tell-tale signs. They may repeatedly mop their brow or tap their fingers, move their leg up and down under the table or blink more frequently. As a chess player I can reveal that when an opponent makes a blunder, he often signals this by going pink behind the ears! Or he might stare over long at a particular piece with a look of anticipation or horror! Such signs may suggest it is a good time to score an important point, or discover a gem of information when the member of the opposite team is somewhat bedevilled. And some may use particular signals by way of a double bluff.

People "speak" with their facial expressions and their utterances. Some can't avoid it whilst others put it to good use. Your facial expression may indicate total frustration or annoyance, or indicate your opposite number has gone too far. Or a willing encouraging smile may be reciprocated as you get ever nearer a mutually satisfactory outcome. But beware, if your opposite number detects your smile of satisfaction, he may come back for more concessions on the strength of it! If language can get in the way of simple courtesies, it can certainly impact on negotiations. At a dinner once in France I said "thank you" when asked if I wanted a glass of wine, and the person serving moved on to the next guest and I was left out! Seemingly "yes please" would have been appropriate as my answer meant I was not in need. And when I declined more food by saying I was "plein," the term to indicate you need your petrol tank filled, I was in fact indicating I was full in a different way. I was pregnant!

A simple grunt can say "not on your life," "no thank you," or "I'll consider it!" A nod might indicate acceptance. Saying nothing whatever can be just as cogent. The non-spoken word in "negotiating language" it seems is inexhaustible. But don't get too obsessed with spotting these signs at the cost of distracting yourself from the essential purpose in hand.

## Presentation and Progress

Adopt an air of confidence throughout. A good many executives go to some lengths to create an air of prestige. This may be in their dress or in the car they drive for example. I personally abhor this attitude but it has always been rife in the West Midlands, the home of so much car production over the years. And when two strangers meet for the first time, and the immediate conversation turns to the car they drive, it does nothing for me! I drove a very handsome car when serving one group as its chief executive to give the impression we were no more impoverished or less successful than my predecessor who drove a very expensive Porsche! And it was the common belief that this was quite an essential signal we were obliged to give! What nonsense but it seems to be a fact of life which you should certainly not allow to impact on your confidence in the negotiating room. In my next job interview I turned up in that very same car and it so obviously upset the chairman of that organisation when I parked next to his less ambitious model it served as a hindrance. A more productive way of boosting your prestige is through the standard of your printed material, the models you have to illustrate your product, the manner in which guests are received at your premises and other considerations you will be well versed with.

As best you can hide your emotions. Show them positively if in doing so consolidates a position. Don't crow over minor victories along the way, nor look smug as it won't help your cause. A smile can work in both directions but I am inclined to be both confident and positive and do not as a rule ignore the consolidating value a smile can bring.

Good negotiators are like good salesmen and some get up to all manner of little tricks. A firm selling windows may meet a potential buyer at the door, but take him the long way around to the negotiating room so as to pass a showpiece with a view to pausing for discussion. Or the product may already be so popular that the only matter in contention is the price.

It doesn't serve you well to enter discussions saying you are "prepared to negotiate" because that means you will have surrendered ground in the first sentence. A neighbour has recently put his house on the market and on the first day ran an advert saying the price was "negotiable!"

There is no way on Earth he will now meet his price unless there is very fierce competition. Even that has its opposite equivalent in the hands of estate agents when they fix the price at a giveaway level to attract hordes. As part of this device, they offer a single viewing day for the numbers the tactic attracts, and then seek to have them compete amongst each other until the real target price is reached or exceeded. Closed bids in sealed envelopes are often stipulated in such examples, often with considerable success.

If you are going to make a concession then drag it out and make it hard won. If you have a bottom-line stick to it, remembering you don't have to agree to anything. And challenge anything you consider misrepresented. Take notes of what is agreed as you go along, especially at key points so as to underline and emphasise the point. And follow up with a written confirmation at the earliest opportunity.

Learn what works for you, where you have had successes in the past and how you achieved them. Look back at your most recent negotiations and consider if you might have done better employing one or other of the many such ploys included herein. As a means of sharpening your mind such a review can do no harm. Every success will sit along the others to enhance your bottom-line results.

Expect to have to make compromises. Without them you are not likely to reach agreement. Remember you are seeking that win-win situation when both parties can leave the meeting feeling satisfied.

Be very conscious that there are many considerations other than price, such as quality, after service, the guarantee period, technical specification, prospects of reciprocal business and a good many more which come into play. And when you get down to price it's always best not to play your hand by asking about this in a hurry. Instead focus on the other aspects such as those included above. Be ready for the inevitable attempts to criticise the product or service, and a little like a game of ping-pong, your technique of deflecting such attempts.

# Chapter 4
# Tactical Ploys

We have already encountered some regularly used ploys and this chapter will now focus on the remaining range of tactics utilised to good effect, whether this be between individuals or teams of dedicated negotiators.

Just about the most common ploy you will ever meet is that old chestnut of the "other party." You are told your price is too high and that some other party, imagined or otherwise, is offering the same product or service at a lower price. Before you even respond to this be aware that price is only one factor that gives value to a product, and be prepared to emphasise all the other good aspects of your product that the customer needs to take into account.

So long as you can demonstrate your customer is getting good value for money the actual price assumes much less significance.

So far as the price itself is concerned you should always be aware of your competition so you can repudiate any false claims. If you are really hungry for business you might make a token reduction, but not immediately if you feel the assertion is valid. But ask yourself, if the customer can obtain the product or service cheaper elsewhere, what is he doing discussing it with you!? By far the best way to call a bluff is to suggest you have urgent matters at hand. Recommend his best option in the circumstances is to buy from the other party, but not before you point out all the other favourable features of your product beforehand which would deter him from doing so. You may lose a little business here and there but if your counterpart is bluffing then this response will leave him embarrassed and in conciliatory mood. You might even be in a position to announce a future price increase to him on the back of his climb down!

As a ploy in its own right the announcement of future price increases or other changes in terms can serve you very well. This can work as a very trusted tactic by way of a rebuttal to those demanding discounts. Buy now, or face a price increase, is a well-recognised market position.

Sometimes a customer will arrive in an accusative mood complaining that some aspect or other of your product has let him down. Every business has hiccups from time to time, and if he is right, you should treat him with courtesy and undertake to sort the matter out. But on no account let him think he has browbeaten you down by attacking the reputation of your product simply as a negotiating tactic.

A fiery business colleague of mine you will read about later had a rather unconventional way of treating his customer on one occasion when the customer hurled verbal abuse at him rather loudly down the phone line. He asked him his whereabouts and marched directly around there to floor him with one punch. As he departed, he left a note on the table giving the details of a rival competitor. He advised his floored opponent, "You'll be needing this!" and stormed out of the room! Not to be recommended!

There are occasions when the supplier can exercise great control over his prices and set them sky high. This happens when a supplier obtains a monopoly grip on the product, and only statutory controls can influence the situation. Or it will be resolved in due course by market forces. But when a supplier decides to cease production of a product, perhaps one that has failed, he is in a special position to bump his prices up on his final production run. A notice will go out to all past customers for the product that it is about to be withdrawn, and the much-elevated price will be communicated. The chances are before the labour employed in that manufacture is withdrawn they will be worked around the clock to build up the stocks through which the company will make a final killing. If the customer has no other convenient alternative at short notice, then there is little he can do about the situation because if he holds off, he runs the risk that there will be no product left.

Perhaps the most vexatious of all positions is when your opposite number sits on the fence and plays the "waiting game." Their tactic is to run you into the ground so that you will finally give in to their demands. In this situation you have three choices. You may not be too inconvenienced if you have a full order book. You may tell them to go away. And if they contend, they have to refer to somebody higher up recognise this for what it is and call their bluff. We have all heard the expression "take me to the organ grinder, not the monkey!" This is not to advocate embarrassing your opposite number with that particular riposte, but the more responsible member of the opposite team will always feel inferior in front of his colleagues faced with such a request, and may suddenly find he does have the power of decision after all!

A variation in the negotiating debate already touched on is to simply "bite your tongue!" When a negotiator is unsure of his position, he is likely to cover this by talking too much. Facing a stone-faced silent executive opposite him he is all the more likely to want to conclude the matter. He will be more inclined to make some concession or other to keep the discussion alive and to move things forward. Under this kind of pressure, he may be inclined to talk too much and in doing so he may reveal valuable information that you can turn to your advantage. As inferred earlier silence can be a real asset when used to good effect by either party!

Ask questions! Every answer will undoubtedly be of value to you. Apart from the value of the information, asking questions puts you in the driver's seat.

Any authority on negotiation will always tell you to strive for that "win-win" situation in which both sides go away well satisfied with the outcome. This must be your fundamental aim throughout so if you can see for yourselves that the other side is not getting much out of the discussions then you should, as a deliberate tactic, strive to find something he will value at least cost to yourselves. And remember that there is always the prospect of more business down the line if relationships are good.

In any team, or duo, there will be personalities which complement each other. There is usually one who is stern and uncompromising whilst one is more understanding and giving. Finance directors are often painted as the stern members of a team, and not without good reason since they are always acutely aware of the impact. Marketing executives are the more likely ones, it is commonly held, to be generous and more sympathetic. Theirs is the responsibility for selling, and they are ever more conscious of future business coming down the line. And such pairings can work very well. The sterner executive will set the bar high and his colleague will repair any damage done to relationships as the negotiations progress. Working together they can steadily improve their position, for if no great harm is done by the former colleague, then the later has no need to repair the damage and the bar set by the sterner member holds.     By repeating this kind of progress, the optimum result may be obtained. The parties may not even be conscious of what is happening! As you read through the case studies you will see how I paired off with a baronet on our team who was an out and out marketing man in negotiations with the Kenco coffee company. And another example was when in South Africa I paired off with another out and out marketing man who managed our subsidiary there.

Your aim should always be to get the maximum deal, not merely an adequate one. Towards this end make much of all the desirable features you have on offer. Talk them up but at the same time talk down what the opposite party or the competition has to offer. Remember that you are striving to enhance the overall mix of high yielding projects in your operation. Each one that is better than the one before will raise the average performance, and this cannot be repeated enough. By the same definition the opposite is equally true as has also been stated.

But having said that it is a sound tactic not to win "too well." If the other party feels you have unnecessarily ground him into the earth, then his resentment may do you more harm in the long term. Always exercise your judgement.

Let's suppose you reach a "stale mate" situation when insoluble problems bring any progress to an end. Somewhere there will be a bottleneck. If it is caused by external factors then both parties should combine their resources to try and resolve the matter. If it is within the power of the parties to resolve the issue between themselves, we come to that most quintessential of all tactics, namely "the compromise!" It is extremely rare for any negotiation to take place without one or other, or both, parties having to compromise. You may set your terms artificially higher in anticipation of this inevitability so that the end result is what you desire all along, but you can't over milk this for obvious reasons. And this brings us back to that "British compromise" that we have already discounted as being of reduced value. It is a matter of keen judgement what compromises are found, but once agreed both parties can leave satisfied with the outcome. If you feel you are the party giving most ground then do make much of it. It will only enhance your position in future such discussions.

But you may be advised to negotiate on the basis of "closed bidding," authentic or invented, and touched upon earlier. As a tactic as such you may suggest that your opposite number is facing competition from another, or a number, of parties. You may invite him to make a bid in a sealed envelope to be delivered on a certain day when in fact no other parties need necessarily exist! You can always communicate that the reserve level set for the transaction has not been exceeded and walk away if the ruse fails! Such skulduggery certainly exists in the world of negotiation and should never be overlooked.

If your opposite number is getting a raw deal, he is inevitably going to feel a deep sense of embarrassment, such that the negotiations may grind to a halt. A very traditional means of overcoming such a situation is to find that "face saver" that will give him something to crow over and cover any embarrassment he may feel, especially with his peers. The "face saver" is one of the most employed and successful of all negotiating tactics and is an excellent means of enabling your counterpart to hold his head up high. If you can give him some advantage to boast about, real or conceived, then you will hopefully engender a feeling of success all around. As before look for something that is of least cost to yourselves, but some aspect which most obviously carries significance to his business. And it is very often in matters of public interest involving political affairs that the "face saver" carries most weight.

Don't forget to make a show of taking notes of what is agreed, both for practical reasons and to emphasise to the other side what you or they have given ground on.

The common use of an agent is seen as just routine, but it can and should be employed as a tactic in its own right. If your opposite number cannot question you directly, or read your facial reactions, then he cannot turn that knowledge to his advantage. Your position is not weakened in any way. You can give your go between strict instructions determining how far he can deviate from your terms, and the other party has to go to extra lengths at his own risk to discover your position. You are not under any obligation to budge one iota from your path and you hold all the strings. Many do not fully appreciate how this can be played and just what good protection it affords you.

Common is the establishment of the grouping together of several individuals who complement each other's needs. If they obtain a firm grip, you might well call them a "cartel." Not infrequently I encountered roving cliques of non-executive directors. They each appointed the others to sit on their particular boards where they would feel naturally obliged to back them up should any contentious matters arise.

Introducing an "alibi" is a tactic you may encounter. Some external factor or authority may be given as a reason why one party contends it can't move on one matter or another. External regulations may be a good example. They may be served up to avoid giving ground on a particular aspect or they may be used as one element of a "go slow" tactic. You should recognise these issues when you see them, research them thoroughly for the avoidance of doubt, and take advice if necessary before considering how best to deal with them. And if they are being exploited by way of a bluff then simply call the bluff.

Don't be caught for a fool! Any party employing go-slow tactics may well be holding parallel talks behind your back with a third party. Flush this out by any means and bring the subject up directly when you feel this is in your interest.

Such a party might only be negotiating with you in the first place to try and unearth technical secrets of value to them or a third party. They may be using ground gained with you to bargain with another party, and vice versa. If they show too keen an interest in touring your manufacturing processes consider carefully what harm might come of it before agreeing to take them anywhere near.

An over employed but key tactic is the "walk away" which can happen at any time in the course of the negotiations but is even more effective if this happens when all else has been exhausted by one side or the other. The other side has not got the best deal it was seeking and feigns a position in which it will walk away from any further discussions. Recognise this for what it is. Don't waste further time on the matter unless truly crucial, and again use your judgement before reacting.

Negotiate always within the framework of the law, and if you are asked to agree to anything which you feel would be outside the law then simply saying so is always your best approach.

Not always so much a tactic as a necessity follows the "adjournment" You may reach a legitimate situation where an adjournment is not a ploy but quite necessary, and there is no harm in this. Indeed, it may be the only plausible way of making any progress. Rushed negotiations can often result in subsequent disappointment on both sides. In seeking that win-win position with both parties feeling they have succeeded it is important the other side leaves feeling it has been a hard-won victory. Anything else will harbour doubts that they might have done better. Avoid this at all costs!

The "last minute" tactic can be very effective and also very frustrating! Just when you think you have arrived at a satisfactory conclusion the other side introduces a last-minute demand for the first time! Your counter tactic should be to dismiss it as too late and irrelevant if possible, failing which be certain to ask for an equal and opposite concession from the other side.

"Slowing the rush to price agreement" is good advice. Price should almost be the last thing you discuss in complex negotiations. If you bring the question of price to a head too early in the negotiations you will lose the opportunity of winning concessions on just about everything else. And reverting back to the issue of price itself don't respond to a request for a price reduction too easily. Never make it seem easy. It has to be hard won after much murmuring and expressions of concern. Stall for time and leave considerable doubt as to whether you might comply until the last moment if you have to yield at all. Don't rush to a conclusion over price.

The negotiations may be so long and complex that you can only take bite sized steps at a time, as in the case for example of the Government's major HS2 project for a fast rail link between London and the north to give another example. In such huge transactions there are always more than just two teams of negotiators involved in the many aspects that have to be covered so this is another case in point when an adjournment is often the only way forward.

"Co-operation" is the most valuable and underrated tactic employed in defending your position against major public and international bodies. Later in the book I deal with what amounted to vital negotiations with the European Union. There will always be some ongoing situations to encounter with the EU it seems, but the example given is of the same relevance to other situations with such strong public and international bodies that you are likely to encounter around the world.

And using "anticipation" and "cunning" helped me obtain the opening of nothing less than a railway station in a small village in Hertfordshire back in 1981 as you will read about later in the book. In this case my point of liaison was necessary with numerous separate authorities before we finally succeeded. Constant adjournments were the norm rather than the exception. This should not be taken as any kind of failure but merely business as usual to be taken in your stride.

These are just those tactics that most readily come to our attention, but there are without doubt others that my reader will have encountered in this rich tapestry of commerce and business and in their private lives. Remember that sometimes the best negotiation is to agree to disagree, and part friends. There is no fun in shooting yourself in the foot! Never let "negotiation fever" get a grip on you when the process of the debate is more important than the substance!

It is important that you don't get into the habit of commenting out loud on the progress being made, as you conceive it, before the deal is concluded. If you hint, for example, that you are "nearly there" this may be a statement of fact that will have no impact – but you could on the other hand be giving signals that you are about to submit. You may simply encourage the opposite party to go one step further in seeking more concessions. I feel instinctively that if somebody were to say to me "we were nearly there" I would be scratching around to think of what further concession I might be seeking! These types of phrases are auto suggestive and it's best to steer a straight unwavering course avoiding them!

But, as with most of the tactics here mentioned, the opposite applies very often with equal force. All the tactics referred to can be used as part of your armoury in a positive sense, or alternatively against your counterpart on the other hand.

Pick up on give-away comments, interpret what they mean and turn them to your own advantage!

There is a corollary to not "winning too well" and that is to say if you feel you have lost a project, then lose graciously.

## Diverting the Subject

You may be pushed on matters to do with a running negotiation that you do not want to discuss, and then particular tactics may be necessary to divert the issue. Nothing is worse than having to respond to press enquiries after an event takes place or company results are announced. The best course of action is to simply state that you have made your public statement and have nothing further to say. But experience has taught me that devious reporters will never leave it at that. They always want to squeeze a bit more out of you, or even worse trip you up by putting words into your own mouth. Deny them and they will threaten to publish the opposite. The tactics employed are often quite underhanded.

This kind of negotiation over what the press is going to report can be very damaging, and you have to proceed with great caution. Whatever else you do appoint just one experienced person to handle such calls. Caution all other members not to engage them in conversation at their peril!

I was always amused at the tactics my chief executive used on the rare occasion he accompanied me to a bank meeting. Given he had literally hundreds of directorships, many of which were with major plc companies, he invariably responded to a question with a tale relevant to one of his other interests! Of course, this was not what the bank wanted to hear so they had the task of constantly trying to get him back on track. I generally knew what kind of answer would placate the manager and came to the rescue. In time the manager usually diverted the conversation into more personal matters and the pressure was off.

It also helped if I chipped in with some titbit of the latest technological advancements. A favourite was the "slumping" of variable lenses, a very interesting manufacturing method we were experimenting with in Germany at the time wherein lens blanks were "cooked" in an oven and slumped over a mould to produce perfect variable lenses in result in quantity. That kind of story always accounted for anything up to twenty minutes or so and relieved the tension ahead of the next question.

## Chance Negotiations

We have been mostly concerned with negotiations held in meetings between individuals or teams, or a mix of both. But a great many negotiating opportunities or obligations can happen anywhere any time by chance. Such a situation for example would be the chance meeting of two executives on the train from Brighton to Waterloo. Such a chance meeting might present an unexpected opportunity to discuss a new deal, or it might put you on the spot when you would prefer to avoid the issue at all costs.

You will read later how my chairman made a deliberate off-the-cuff remark to the Pilkington glass company that resulted in our having to fight for our very existence. There are many ways you can "test the temperature" without much consequence, but you are entering dangerous territory as you will discover. Chance meetings are most certainly a time of greatest potential risk. You are away from your desk, and from your carefully rehearsed script. You are in unfamiliar surroundings with no colleagues to refer to for assistance. And it is just your bad luck to run into the last person you wanted to meet who fires direct questions at you on the spot! The author once ran into a senior member of a stockbroker company earlier the same day the public results were to be announced. He had supported the company strongly and consistently and felt I was obliged to give him an advance insight into what would be announced later in the day. But to do so would be an offence under the insider trading laws. When you are caught short like this, you have to be prepared, and keep to your convictions whatever the outcome.

## Mandatory Negotiations

You may find yourself summoned to attend a meeting by somebody with requisite authority, in which case the location and tenor of the meeting will be out of your control.

The proceedings are usually very formal and not something to be looked forward to with enthusiasm. The author was once called to a customs and excise meeting over an issue concerning the incorrect completion of a value added tax form by his staff. It was held in a soulless dark office by a sharply spoken miserable looking official. Each word was taken down in shorthand by a stenographer in an atmosphere suggesting we were about to be thrust into handcuffs on the spot! That was bad enough but things got worse when I was asked to identify my signature on a document and recognised it to be false. It had been forged by one of my staff in my absence, I was told, for expediency!

Being asked to attend court or some other official hearings are further examples that occur to me.

There are some situations that are quite specialised and I discuss these further on. These will include such matters as takeovers, takeover defences and management buyouts.

All of the tactics and ploys we have touched on in this summary you will encounter in the following pages, and recognise them for what they are. They are part of real-life examples drawn from my own experience over a good many years since my journey into top business began from such unlikely beginnings. I hope you will find them all of interest, even entertaining, but above all else useful.

Some tactics may suit you better than others. Most you will already be familiar with, but there will be nothing lost by reviewing them and rekindling your interest. You will be surprised just how many such tactics and ploys abound in negotiations, simple and complex. I have pet names for them that are suggestive of their nature, and I list below a summary of key words to help you identify them in the form of a checklist.

"Not negotiable"
"The red line"
"The other party"
"The complainer and the put down"
"The unspoken word"
"Facial signals and vocal antics"
"Elevating prices to meet discount demands"
"The British compromise"
"The waiting game"
"Biting your tongue"
"Asking questions"
"Questioning authority to close a deal"
"Striving for the win-win outcome"
"Working in complementary pairs"
"Getting the very best deal"
"Talking up, talking down"
"Winning too well"
"Stale mate, and the brick wall"
"The compromise"
"The all-important face saver"
"The phantom face saver"
"Taking notes as a tactic"
"The go-between, or agent"
"The alibi"
"Calling the bluff"
"Using bluff"
"The spy and intelligence gathering"
"The adjournment"
"Last minute demands, and the riposte"
"Raising your wants"
"The counter offer"
"Playing hard to get"
"Public body co-operation"
"Impending price increases"
"The diversion"
"give-away comments"

"The chance meeting"

"The off the cuff remark"

"Fishing or testing the temperature"

"Employing legal constraints"

"Engendering goodwill"

"The walk away"

"Mandatory attendance, and the co-operative mode"

"Closed bidding"

"Setting the mood"

"fait accompli"

"The take-over defence"

"The management buy-out"

"The no-deal"

You will encounter them all as you read further through the case studies I have been personally involved with. As we said at the outset, negotiation is necessarily present in all strands of our business and personal lives, of fundamental importance to both. No thorough writing on the subject can focus only on one or the other so you will find examples that concern both in all walks of life.

The chapters are arranged to start with some lighter examples biased more towards our personal lives. As you progress through the book you will find issues that assume far greater significance for business. They will range from the defence of your independence to dealing with public bodies and specialist areas such as management buyouts. To re-emphasize the tactics discussed you should aim to recognise for yourself as you read on through the pages. I earnestly hope that in doing so you will be stimulated to recall and refresh your experiences, and enlarge and consolidate your own negotiation armoury.

A summary of a number of the main points is made at the foot of each section by way of an aide memoir.

# Chapter 5
# Haggling

With the advent of such easy travel today throughout the globe millions of people have experienced what it is to haggle with local traders over the price of souvenirs and goods they bring back home. And the ever-growing popularity of cruising has added to the numbers arriving in far off places considerably. The quantity of souvenirs I have personally brought home simply amazes me now as I look back. And I marvel at just how I brought some items back simply given the pure size of them. The only souvenir that got away was a pair of amazingly hand-crafted drums from Zimbabwe, each one a meter or more wide and deep into the bargain. They could neither be carried nor dispatched through the post at the time, even were it not for the fear of disease being spread through the skins. But how I brought home my carving of a Maasai warrior, which stands as high as my thighs for example, I can't now imagine! Nor that of my giant carving of elephants on a copper base, of which more later. Suffice to say there is more than enough mouth-watering temptation to haggle for souvenirs when abroad that a chapter devoted to the method is more than justified.

Many millions today are familiar with arriving at a faraway place to find traders waiting to haggle for their goods. When I look back at some of the amazing deals I have struck, I sometimes now feel a sense of guilt that I drove the price down so far. But then again on the one occasion when I didn't haggle, the trader heaped abuse on me for not having done so! He regarded it as some kind of insult! If haggling is the system ingrained in the country, it seems they respect you less if you don't haggle!

The traders will already have determined how low they are prepared to go, and nobody is forcing them to agree to anything. Rather they rely on your trade and you won't get value for money unless you adopt the system they are all used to. Safe to say that in various places they adopt a fixed price system which is heavily enforced. That simplifies things a great deal and saves you time, whilst at the same time denying you the pleasure! But when you are engaged in haggling you may, as I have done over the years, encounter some outstanding characters, and have enormous fun along the way. I have been in situations when I didn't feel disposed to haggle and, either through disappointment or naivety, they have commenced haggling against their own interests on my behalf!

So how to conduct yourself in such a situation to obtain the best result? I find that if you browse around and spot something you take a fancy to then give yourself distance immediately. Glance around at anything else on view but never show any real interest in your quarry. He or she will probably have been observant enough to spot that momentary hesitation and will soon approach you. Walk away! Nothing is ever quite so effective! And when you might wander back nonchalantly the trader will be keen to tie you down. Ask casually about the price for something you have no interest in, and only after moving along enquire about the price of your target. And of course it follows the time-honoured way in which the trader will quote a price and you respond with a counter offer well below that you expect to pay. As the haggling process continues the gap between you narrows at which point the trader is likely to tell you his "last price." Hesitate further and he will ask you "what is your last price?" Facial expressions of disappointment, claims you have not enough cash on your person, walking away to return again to clinch a final deal are all tools of the trade. And you finally do your deal.

If the place you are visiting is somewhat boring then this is as good a way of idling time away I find than anything else. Better than being driven off to the same beach you have visited umpteen times before to be sat in countless rows of visitors denying you any view of the sea whatever! That is unless you happen to be a sun worshipper! These days when you get there you will almost certainly encounter a local rushing up to direct you to your sun chair and sunshade for his set fee. But back at the docks you get that second chance to haggle for that carved elephant or whatever else took your eye! If you are about to board your cruise ship and depart you will commonly find the trader more amenable than when you last left him, and finally get your bargain price. Perhaps the best place to strike a good deal is just before you board your ship. I bought a watch once on the third step up as I was boarding the ship, the watch being held by us both and the notes I had offered being extended towards the seller. Only at the last minute did he release the watch and conclude the deal by accepting the amount I had offered.

Whilst in Egypt with my daughter a young trader, who obviously admired her, passed her what he called a "present" though the window of the coach. Once she treasured it to her person he announced the price in a very astute piece of negotiation, but as the coach left, she refused either to pay the price nor return the "present" and still has it today. It was after all a present she told him! They were trying to entice young women to take a ride on a camel, which, once boarded is not by any means the easiest beast to dismount. Miles into the desert the frightening custom at the time was to demand a "ransom," a horrible piece of negotiation whichever way they dressed it up. Only on payment would they then return her to her family.

And on a boat trip in Togo approaching a far distant island, the other side of a huge lake, the rowers stopped halfway to negotiated (for which read demand) an extra fee to continue rowing. They were too exhausted to row any further without an additional payment! The trip had the sense of Dr Livingstone about it as we approached the native settlement on the far-off shores. Once there a rush of natives ran into the water greeting us with spears waved frighteningly above their heads in the air. In the event it turned out they wanted a dollar to carry individuals from the boats to shore whilst keeping them dry, whether you wanted such an escort or not! It took four of them to carry a rather portly lady ashore, squealing her head off as her many petticoats flared in the wind!

Of course there is an investment in your own time in buying a simple item such as a shirt, and you can spend too much time haggling over the last cent when others are waiting to pursue their holiday interests. My son once tired of my extended efforts to knock a few cents of what was already a bargain price on one occasion, so he settled the matter by buying some himself in front of my very eyes at the asking price! An abrupt end to the haggling probably well warranted.

What I find unreasonable in non haggling situations is the practice of not showing a price on the product at all. Worse, when haggling is the norm being asked what you are prepared to pay when you have no idea of it's true worth. Shopping around so that you are able to quote competitive prices from other sources is perhaps the best antidote for this situation. But watch also the real value of what you are buying. It's the easiest thing in the world to come away with something said to be of one rare stone or another, or a carving in precious wood, only to find the stone is rubbish and the wood on closer examination merely plaster cast in a mould. What you thought was a sound negotiation turns out to be a complete disappointment!

Once in Nairobi, Kenya I became very interested in two carved wooden figures of Maasai warriors in feathers and sporting swords in full fighting regalia. I tried the price for one first, then asked for a discount if I should buy them both. Not being satisfied with the result I followed my own advice and walked away only to find myself followed by the trader at every turn from one end of the city to the other. He tried everything. First of all, I was some sort of a villain for having commenced trading without concluding a deal. Then failure to complete the transaction would bring shame on him in the eyes of his family and the community. Next his family might be starving. He might be so desperate he would "kill himself" if he failed in his mission! I have met them all.

Along the way I picked up on the price again and the haggling continued further. After trailing along through numerous streets trying to avoid him, and desperately trying to avoid eye contact, I was beginning to feel the price we were down to was too good to be true. So I tried my luck at one final bid when something occurred that I still chuckle over to this day. I named a lower price and he responded by going even lower to my advantage! So caught up in the bargaining process was he that he was now taking my role and trading against himself! The transaction finally concluded he all but collapsed on the spot from sheer exhaustion. Today my carved warriors sit in my study along with enough African pieces to start a shop in my own right!

On another occasion in Port Said, Egypt, we looked at a quartz vase which was exquisitely made, but we weren't quite sure if we could find a place for it at home amongst so much else. The haggling process came to an end and we decided we had no further interest. We would forgo the pleasure of owning this lovely item. We left and were approaching our cruise ship when we heard a bicycle bell sounding with great enthusiasm, its rider peddling hard and clearly out of breath shouting some message we couldn't quite understand, the quartz vase held high in his hand! Apparently, he would now meet our price and we hadn't the heart to refuse him! His tactic to meet our price whilst banking on our sympathy, if that was his intention, was a clear success even if his muscles would surely ache the next day.

One of the most amusing, but instructive moments, came with a native on a Caribbean Island with the name of Joseph. When abroad I always have an urge to bring back a cassette or disc of local music I rarely ever play again. Joseph was trying to sell us some tapes in a lesser-known part of the Caribbean islands. His negotiating skills were pretty good and I felt he was getting the better of me. Then I directly challenged him and asked why he was charging so much to which he responded, "It was a consequence of the distance from the main town."

I was quick enough to say,

*"Well thank you, Joseph. We will be there tomorrow!"*

This caused considerable amusement and not least on the part of our new friend, Joseph! In the list of tactical ploys in the previous chapter we spoke of "the other party." In this instance it was the town itself that served as the other party! Today whenever anybody shoots themselves in the foot we say, "He has done a Joseph!" Little does Joseph know that a whole saying in our vocabulary has been created at his expense! And of course the negotiating trick in this instance is just to be sharp, use your wits and always look out for such opportunities. Recognise such hostages to fortune and turn them to your advantage.

Turning your pockets out and claiming you have no more cash than that offered on your person can work wonders, providing you can convince the other party you are not telling fibs!

On one occasion we were haggling over the price of a beautiful bird carved out of a semi-precious stone in Rio when a woman leaned over, snatched the object from our very grasp, and offered to bid above us! We were speechless at her bold aggression, and have never quite got over the experience! We have always bemoaned the negotiation that got away!

Not so far removed from haggling is the practice of barter and, in like manner, exchange. At its most simplistic level you can imagine somebody with a surplus of bread exchanging this for rice wherein both parties have to decide what value they place on each, what is surplus to their requirements, and at what quantity a deal might be struck.

Or music lovers who have tired of their rock music might exchange their own with another for some classical recordings. In the Stone Age, who knows, perhaps wives were exchanged for spears or a square meal, but that wouldn't be a popular sentiment today and rightly so! Perhaps the reverse applied!

And at a more commercial level we were once faced with dividend controls wherein we could not bring any profits from an overseas subsidiary back home.

But what we could do was bring in their ample stocks of coffee for sale through our coffee services subsidiary hence avoiding the outlay elsewhere.

### Key Tactics Summary

Know how to haggle effectively.

Us the tactic of walking away.

Be prepared for the unexpected.

A glance at a product is enough to invite a negotiation.

Don't do a "Joseph" on yourself!

Just say your offer constitutes all the cash you have!

Negotiate a barter or exchange if other avenues are closed.

# Chapter 6
# The Wedding

A couple meet for the first time at a wedding, he the best man and she the chief bridesmaid. The nervous groom made sure the best man was well versed in his responsibilities, and amongst his other duties he would be responsible for looking after the chief bridesmaid. As chance would have it, they clicked, but she lived in Edinburgh and he in England. But as she knew little about her own country, he took delight in showing her around. They visited the romantic Isle of Skye where he proposed. Her parents having died young she had been taken in by an aunt, and she and another aunt fiercely protected her interests. So much so that they became known to him as the "dragons."

As the wedding day approaches, they realise that being of different faiths would present more difficulties than they ever imagined, no doubt exacerbated by the expectations and demands of the "dragons." The wedding was to be held in Edinburgh but the priest refused to carry out the service unless the groom committed to bringing up any children in the Catholic faith. So far as the groom was concerned this was hardly democratic and in fact rather arrogant on the priest's part. But as they were several hundred miles apart negotiating any solution was going to be very troublesome, if not insoluble. An alternate priest local to the groom was appointed to hold a series of meetings to "persuade" him towards their point of view. A series of six meetings had been arranged on successive Sundays by which time the church clearly imagined they would have browbeaten and bullied the young man down. But he was made of sterner stuff. There was no option but to attend each meeting on successive Sundays, but the young man stubbornly refused to be dictated to. Each Sunday he duly turned up, for there was no other choice, and each Sunday he sat and listened to the same old lines and each time he stubbornly refused to be swayed. By the time the final Sunday came around the local priest, who had taken continuous instructions from the officiating one in Edinburgh, made it clear that failure to conform would mean the wedding was off. And the bride-to-be was getting ever anxious. A solution had to be found from somewhere but the church remained adamant, confident they were carrying out God's will. Whilst the groom was alone and at some distance the priests had the authority of their church, and God on their side into the bargain!

It became clear that it would be for the groom to find a way of making some kind of progress. So here was the deal.

Admitting he was not a keen church goer, and would prefer spending his Sundays relaxing after a hectic week, he explained he would want his children to have the opportunity at least of being introduced to religion. He would be happy then for them to make up their own minds over time. He reasoned that his wife was likely to attend her own church, and as a matter of practical expedience he would not stand in her way if that happened to be in a Catholic church, and she took the children with her.

This is one of many examples of using the negotiating technique of "compromise" you will encounter elsewhere in this book, except that it wasn't! In a compromise both parties give ground to some extent, but none had been given by the young man! There was no guarantee whatever that the wife and children would be compelled to attend a Catholic church. But the artificial compromise worked and the wedding service was duly held in Edinburgh. They went to live in a village with no Catholic church and the wife and children in due course attended the local Church of England, the church in which the young man had been christened himself. The priests never got their bullying way. Their demands had been rebutted, but they took the arrangement as a "face saver" they could use to claim some kind of "success." But in reality, they had accepted a "ghost" or "phantom" compromise which was neither holding nor persuasive morally or otherwise!

Now two children later, and holding down a seriously responsible job, the issue arose what, if anything, should be done about having them christened. The groom had been sent off to church as a youngster, sometimes twice on a Sunday but always regarded it as an ordeal. The nearest he came to religion thereafter was the strong spiritual feeling felt somewhere up a mountainside. But time had elapsed and the children had not been christened in any church of any denomination, so the couple discussed this and approached the local Church of England vicar to ask him to perform the ceremony. After all, the couple's son was a leading light by then in the church choir. Yet again the wishes of the family were derailed by the bigotry of this church this time around. Ironically, he wouldn't perform such a ceremony for nothing – the entire family would have to attend each Sunday on a regular basis before he would even consider the request. The children were both consulted and had no strong concerns whether they were christened or not. They had their own doubts but were in no such hurry. So this time the family withdrew from any further deliberations and there was no such conclusion.

Twenty years on and the couple grew apart and agreed to divorce. They follow the advice of all the experts, and in a friendly enough vein negotiated the financial settlement that would satisfy both. That is until the solicitors weighed into the situation and added their own terms to what the woman should accept. Now the atmosphere was tense, and patience was being tested on both sides. The prestige car the groom ran for business purposes was brought into consideration, as was his pension pot, insurances and anything else that may have some intrinsic value. Any further damage would cost him the purchase of the property he had wanted to buy, and there was a limit to how much mortgage he could obtain. But the wife was told she had plenty of years left to build up her own pension pot and this was conceded in return for a very handsome cash settlement. The fairy tale marriage came to an end.

Where are the key negotiating points in this rather sad tale?

Firstly, in any such vexing situation try and agree something. This is standard advice you will receive from any source.

Evaluate your respective assets and liabilities beforehand.

Focus strongly on your priorities. The groom in this case held great store in his pension fund and was prepared to compromise on other aspects of the settlement to retain those rights. As it happened fluke circumstances that followed made his pension pot all the more valuable although this was not known at the time. She would have the facility to buy her own house, and time and money to enhance her own pension pot in view of her young age. Both parties defended what they valued most vigorously. Of all the lessons to learn in such a situation a major consideration is to avoid the solicitors practicing family law fuelling high running emotions by wading into areas already agreed between the couple. So keep a tight rein on such solicitors who all too often seem to think they are a law unto themselves! It has long been contended that they compound arguments to simply justify substantial increases in their fees! Perhaps this may be the case. But during the sad process do draw breath and review matters from time-to-time once legalities are under way.

By way of a confession, I was that groom.

When I was in my 'teens the nearest church was Methodist and we were constantly visited by one Sister Winnifred Booth. She would knock on doors and herd the whole family along for her service. It was on such a visit that my young sister inadvertently pulled off a very convenient negotiation, if this isn't stretching a point too far! Sister Booth, who had problems getting in and out of an armchair because of her weight, was sitting in one when my young sister appeared excitingly to show her a pet white mouse. When she accidentally dropped it in the sister's lap all hell let loose and we were never troubled again. Just goes to show you can negotiate with actions as well as words! Even a small white mouse has it's uses!

### Key Tactics Summary
Use the principle of compromise to resolve an impasse.
If you can't accept a solution, find a "ghost" counteroffer.
Use whatever you can to unlock the impasse.
"Face savers" are your best tool.
Remember you are not bound to negotiate, nor concede.
Reach a mutually agreed position before solicitors become involved.
Don't give in too easily.
Be downright stubborn if you can't give ground.
Don't let solicitors go off on a limb.
There may be safer places to holiday than Skye if you are single!

# Chapter 7
# Your Rights

Businesses and individuals alike have rights bestowed upon them from a myriad of laws passed both nationally and internationally, but unless you are an expert lawyer it is unlikely you will have the knowledge to refer to them in the vast majority of cases when disputes arise. Instead, you are often forced to negotiate what you consider to be reasonable when, with the appropriate knowledge, quoting your legal rights is of itself potentially one of your greatest negotiating tools. Specific rights emanate directly from negotiated agreements as witnessed by the subsequent written contracts drawn up between the parties. Such contracts enshrine in detail exactly what it is that has been agreed, and they form the basis upon which the subsequent actions are performed and adjudicated upon in the event of a dispute. So it follows you will be found wanting if you are unaware of your rights, but having said that they can only be as good as they are written.

Errors and mistakes can be very expensive and there is nothing worse than concluding a sound negotiation only to find in its application that it wasn't so clever and incorporated costly errors. Next only to this are those costly errors that creep into draft contracts that nobody spots prior to signature. Errors in its composition that do not reflect what has been agreed. For this reason alone, it is essential that any business or individual encompasses a vetting stage in which draft contracts are examined on a word-to-word basis, specifically with the objective of avoiding any expensive errors before it is too late. To illustrate this, I will give examples of one or two howlers that have come across my path at the vetting stage.

One such contract landed on my desk one sunny afternoon when the perpetrators had arrived back from a celebration lunch with their opposite numbers. There was a carefree celebratory atmosphere about the place which was understandable since a good deal had been confirmed. That is to say it would have been if only the contract had been prepared conscientiously and with greater care and attention. It confirmed the granting of a special discount year on year to our major customer in return for his loyalty so long as he continued to buy all his needs from ourselves. The contract read in words to the effect that the customer, year on year, would always enjoy a price ten per cent below the average for the preceding year. My first thoughts turned to imagining how this was going to work in practice. And then it occurred to me that, since his own discounted purchases would form part of that calculation, the formula would automatically grant him an ever-higher advantage year on year which was not the intention at all! I had it rewritten to describe the formula as "ten per cent below the average after first excluding his own purchases from the calculation of that average!" There were a few red faces and then the merry band went off to eagerly root out their next conquest. We had come perilously close to giving away discount rights which would have cost us dearly. This experience highlighted to me how every organisation always needs an alert "goalkeeper," that being the role I played on that occasion.

Another case arose when our sales department felt they could enhance their sales by accepting the services of a well experienced marketing organisation. To make the operation effective this organisation wanted to accomplish sales using our own well-known trademarks, and our name. So a negotiated contract landed on my desk giving them just that – the right to have exclusive use of our trademarks and name in support of their sales on our behalf. But on reading the small print I concluded that to sign the contract would be giving away our long-established title to our trademarks, our name, our very birth right without redress! In effect everything that was of key value to our company and which we could never again retrieve. After an earnest word with the chairman the whole idea was shelved, and in due course the marketing operation we had chosen turned out to be based on fraud.

My suspicions were first aroused when their slick negotiator was too gushing over my very modest athletic achievements whilst he himself claimed to be in the top half dozen of his own discipline worldwide! When we enquired when his next competition was due it seemed to be an ever-moving feast, whilst all the time he showered us with praise, no doubt playing for time until we signed the contract. What was at work here was that native sense of distrust that goes a long way when you are negotiating if things just don't seem to add up. This should be noted very seriously and you should never doubt your initial judgement if you have good reason to suspect something is wrong. Failure to spot this and we would have negotiated away our rights to our very identity with no recourse whatever.

Negotiating with authorities in France can be something of a nightmare. Having fallen in love with a property surrounded by forest, a meadow and formal gardens I negotiated a price for the property plus eleven acres, and another separate price for further land owned by the vendor's son, in the region of thirty-three acres. The vendor was canny enough to load the price onto the first of the two contracts. This meant the additional land was priced at a bargain level and I was walking blindly into a huge error in a foreign country.

The property was known locally as the "hunting lodge" and local farmers did indeed come onto the land to hunt deer and boar. A neighbour appeared from time to time with two dogs, I suspected looking for highly valued cépe mushrooms and truffles. They also shot birds which they regarded as a tasty delicacy. Foreigners and Parisians were treated with equal distain so they in turn socialised with each other. A Parisian friend once told me,

*"We are all foreigners down here!"*

In a country where the farmer is "king" the local farmer once asked my colleague,

*"How dare he move into the area!?"*

Other than fashioning a path around the perimeter for jogging, I simply wanted to preserve it as a nature reserve and to enjoy its rich variety of wildlife.

Under the Common Agricultural Policy, the favourable treatment of farmers was most apparent. The more land they acquired the more grants they received, simply for the addition of a few more cows. Machinery could be updated to the most modern at an eye watering price, and discarded machinery lay abandoned in the corner of any field. The same policy gave farmers the right to apply to set aside any independently negotiated contract for the purchase of land in their favour, so long as they met the negotiated price. So by negotiating a very low price for the separate land I found I had shot myself in the foot. The farmer was able, despite assurances to the contrary, to commence proceedings to "steal" our land from under our very noses at the attractive price we had negotiated! The same farmer dumped a lorry full of pig excreta right outside the property of my local friend, a not so tacit negotiation you could say indicating he wanted him to get out of the Corrèze!

At this point said Parisian dropped a mysterious unsigned note through my door "offering to help" me contest the farmers claim to "our land." I suspected from the start that he was using me to fight his own battles and wreak revenge on the farmer, but the note contained substance and in due course we met up and joined forces. We couldn't have known at the time but negotiating error number two was about to be committed when we went together to see a particular lawyer in Brive-la-Gaillarde. He explained that in France there is no such thing as equitable solutions, rather everything is done according to the law book (the modern equivalent of the Code Napoleon) Since the farmer had not filed his claim within the stipulated time period, and was also in breach of other procedural rules, we were informed we had an excellent case. Procedure was everything in France we were assured. The lawyer was impressive and assured us he would personally present our arguments at the requisite Tribunal. I fixed a budget for the exercise beyond which I would not go, and took the plunge whilst my newfound friend remained in the background for fear of repercussions. When it came to the Tribunal the lawyer broke his word and sent in a deputy to represent me who had hardly prepared for the case!

At the Tribunal I wasn't allowed to speak, nor had I much command of the language had I been permitted to do so. But when the chair of the meeting suggested to my stand-in lawyer that my intentions were to "exploit" the land I got the drift of his meaning. To my horror my lawyer merely replied idly in the negative without giving any account of what my genuine intentions towards the land were. Had he said I wanted to preserve nature that alone might have been weighed in the balance. As we approached the conclusion, I heard the chairman utter the word "English" with unconcealed animosity, and I knew there and then that the game was lost! It seems that the French idea of equitable law is not so much to come to a fair judgement by reason of the facts, but instead to "tweak" the modern day "Code Napoleon" to set aside the very technical infringements we were told would win us the case. And of course if they have a predisposition to one party or the other this is where all the tweaking of the written law takes place! The numerous negotiations that had led up to this point were not wasted on me however, and I put them all to good use subsequently. The local farmer stood in the way of the authorities on the question of taking a small parcel of land for the protection of the spring water supply, but I cooperated and as a quid pro quo got permission to build my swimming pool which had otherwise seemed an ambition too far in furtherance of protecting the water supply.

You may well ask what the farmer did with the land subsequently. He felled most of the trees for handsome rewards, and with the land cleared set about claiming his extra grants all paid for out of the funds to which we in the United Kingdom contributed from our taxes. Nature suffered badly as a result of his actions. However, the silver lining came when I eventually sold my property, since to do so with so much land would not have been an easy matter in the UK market, whereas in France prices remained depressed.

Whether in France or elsewhere in the world the principals involved here stand out for themselves, not least the way in which I let my enthusiasm overcome due diligence and careful planning. My only defence was that my other half was, perhaps wisely, pulling against the transaction at the time so I went in headstrong before I lost the opportunity! Had I researched my rights in France more thoroughly beforehand I would have deterred the farmer by arguing the price to be shifted more towards the land value. This would have made his deal less attractive. I would also have been well advised to break that land into smaller parcels such that he would have been dissuaded from buying sections I valued which were of little value to him.

We bought an apartment in Cornwall in a converted water mill. There was a small patio at the rear of the property that was clearly attached to our apartment, and which was shown as such on the selling brochure and on the plans. But errors had been made in these documents and the patio was found to be part of the common land to all the apartments in the development. It didn't matter over much until we came to sell and our purchasers were not prepared to exchange contracts without title to the patio area per se.

So I negotiated with the family concerned and was given time to find a solution. There was no management company or structure governing the block of apartments so no further progress could be made until one was formed.

I first held a meeting with the freeholder, a pleasant enough gentleman whose family it seemed had owned half the freeholds in the village for hundreds of years. Since the patio to his mind had always been regarded as the property of our vendor who had developed it, he saw no problem in transferring it to us for a peppercorn sum. But this had to happen before the transfer of the remainder of the land into the newly formed management company or it would have been lost forever. The sequence of the transactions therefore was all important, and the dissenting neighbour next door had legal redress to challenge the transfer if he were so minded. For our part we just kept straight faced and our heads low whilst day after day passed and no challenges came. The specific plot duly transferred, the remainder of the common land was assigned into the newly formed management company, and the deed was done. By this means we duly sold our apartment without further hitch and the problem had been successfully overcome. A long time after our interest in the property had ceased other disputes arose which were settled within the framework of the management company we had created, and for which we were duly thanked. It had performed well as the legal structure within which all negotiated disputes could be settled, and without which each property owner would be left floundering to take his or her own legal action. The point of this anecdote is that there is nearly always a solution to be negotiated given imagination and determination. Once the errors in the originating documents were unearthed our genuine rights were discovered so you can't take everything on trust. In regard to the misrepresentation in the agents details compensation was sought and paid and the matter finally resolved.

When we bought an apartment in Barnet, Hertfordshire we were satisfied that the lease was long enough to represent good value, but we assumed that the tenants in this fairly affluent area would be wanting to extend their leases in the not-too-distant future. This was the acknowledged good practice since mortgage companies are loathe to finance purchases of leases when the period left on the lease is below a given number of years. Without extending the period remaining on the leases this would therefore serve as an impediment to their sale, and we took it for granted there would be no objection to extending them for this very obvious reason. But little did we know!

We were met on the first day by an aggressive petite elderly lady with white hair who announced herself as the "residents chairperson!" She barked orders to us to be sure to clear the remnants of the bits and pieces we had taken in from the stairway, and made it pretty clear that she thought that what she said was law! We let the apartment out by way of an investment so that a succession of different short-term tenants occupied it, much to the dismay of the residents who wanted to maintain exclusivity. And she had studied the Articles almost as a fetish with this objective in mind. So when we let out to a couple about to be married, she flew immediately to the freeholder to complain that an unmarried couple were in the premises, being ultra vires to the fussy Articles!

And on another occasion, she referred the freeholder to a clause banning any billboards appearing at windows when the daughter of one tenant had placed her music score up against the window from the inside! We received a seven-day notice to cause the tenants to take it down, and were obliged to drive down to Barnet from a considerable distance to discover just what the fuss was about.

This fierce little lady was negotiating with the freeholder to wreak vengeance on anybody in the block that did not carry out her bidding, and he was as enthusiastic as she since he stood to profit from any leases he could repeal to add to his growing number of such properties he had successfully redeemed. It transpired through an article in the Sunday Times that the freeholder worked strictly within the letter of the law, but was causing misery to hundreds of leaseholders to his own advantage. The more infamous he became the more the little old lady admired him! And of course he would be the freeholder with whom we would have to negotiate when it came to extending the lease. Whilst in the day the law provided for leaseholders to be given the first opportunity to buy freeholds, this was seldom enacted, and our infamous friend was one of a number that bought up any freeholds he could get his hands on with the express intention of milking the tenants. This often-included notices to bring properties up to their original standard, and when the cost of such a major exercise was beyond tenants, he carried out the repairs through contractors and evicted the tenants for failure to meet the cost, the result being the properties fell into his lap at least cost.

So we were up against this infamous individual as well as the fierce old lady, and to make matters worse she had the support of a semi-retired solicitor in the same block who also had the same jaundiced approach to any owners that let their apartments out. Their sole objective was to keep the block "residents only" and drive us and anybody else who sub-let their apartment out. But there was no way we were going to oblige by selling on and leaving our newly acquired luxury apartment. So after updating myself on our rights I determined the only option was going to be to buy back the freehold. As tenants the law gave us the right to acquire it at an agreed price, failing which a fair price would be determined by a Tribunal. The shorter the term left on the lease the greater would be the price the Tribunal would determine had to be paid, so time was of the essence and we were facing a brick wall. Our decision to fight was the trigger point for a serious of discrete negotiations that would run and run.

You might have thought it a simple matter to obtain a majority of tenants who favoured extending their leases, if only in self-interest, but this couldn't be further from the truth and not least because any neutrals were terrified of the twin force of the old lady and her accommodating solicitor friend, not to mention the freeholder! For others their life expectancy was short and they were simply not bothered at any cost.

I wrote to the chairperson asking for a meeting to discuss the purchase of the freehold, but got a very terse response to the effect that "the resident's committee" was totally opposed to any such scheme, and was not prepared therefore to hold any such meeting. Now first of all the "resident's committee" didn't exist as a legal entity, and secondly as tenants we had a legal right to summon such a meeting. This was obviously going to prove to be a tough one, and it was fast becoming another case of "one against the rest"

Next a piece of good fortune. A younger couple moved into the apartment next opposite ours and were fairly easily converted to the idea. Then an elderly lady I had spoken to, who was almost too terrified to converse, took the opportunity to confess to me she could be interested in my proposal. Furthermore, she had spoken to her friend in the apartment below who was also interested, but not without swearing me to secrecy in the first instance. The name of the negotiating game here was clearly going to be to discretely win one tenant over at a time until, almost without notice, there would finally be a groundswell in favour. But there was still some distance to go.

It seemed that the strength of the "resident's committee" depended in large part on the duality of the chair and the semi-retired solicitor. So my next move was to write a formal letter to him reminding him that as a solicitor, of all occupations, he would be breaking the law if we were not granted the right to discuss the matter in meeting. We duly got our meeting and little by little achieved our ambitions. We finally gained a clear majority and met the price determined by the Tribunal and got the extended leases we had fought so hard to achieve. Without acquainting ourselves with our rights no negotiations could have taken place, and there would have been no satisfactory outcome.

At another time and place in a listed old property, one of fifteen surrounding a courtyard, a debate ensued as to whether ugly concrete slabs should be replaced with block paving or cobbles. The management company had already determined to spend a very considerable sum on simply replacing concrete slabs with the same, without adding any value to the courtyard or the properties within it.

Our late intervention was unwelcoming and we were as good as told it was in the hands of the directors who in turn had been appointed by the shareholders, and we should therefore, to coin a phrase "butt-out!" It seemed to me that a considerable sum was being more or less wasted on installing more of the same when the opportunity had arisen to obtain better value for money. Moreover, the directors announced their decision without discussing it fully with all members in meeting, so it was not therefore put to a vote of shareholders.

My only redress to this protectionism within our structure was to remind them that the company's act does not grant directors carte blanche to do just what they want without regard to shareholders. That it is fully within the rights of a shareholder to raise a concern when material sums are being invested, and such a shareholder should expect both a courteous response and a hearing. Even if that contention might be challenged there were no takers willing to do so, and the directors were obliged to eat humble pie and give proper consideration to the matter. The ability to be able to quote the company's act in this manner changed the course of the matter, which in ignorance of the provisions would otherwise have been completely lost. The clique running the management company would have succeeded and in doing so entrenched their position even more so.

It never fails to astonish me how members of management companies, and others, seem to think that a simple majority can always prevail just because the greater number support a decision. And that without any regard for the Articles of the Company, or the law in general. In regard to another property one resident proposed in my absence our apartment should carry a surcharge to cover the extra cost of wear and tear caused by paying holiday makers in the summer period. This was factually untrue but there was no such provision in the Articles backing such a move, yet it was carried and an invoice carrying a surcharge of thirty per cent landed on my doorstep! A reading of the Articles showed I would have to commence Arbitration proceedings which I was obliged to do within a limited time scale to obtain any remedy to the situation. I did so and the decision was coyly acknowledged and reversed, but had I not been on the ball I could have been stuck with this iniquitous decision. A relatively simple case of knowing your rights and going through the correct procedure saved the day!

**Key Tactics Summary**

Take care what rights you bestow on others.

Protect your trading rights at all costs.

Know your rights or research them if you do not.

Avoid having to take rear-guard action.

Know the different character of rights and practices overseas.

Beware pitfalls.

Don't be easily led on.

Beware old ladies with a power complex!

Beware of rogue freeholders.

Defend your rights against management cliques.

Stand up to bullies.

Consider their rights, but protect your own.

Don't win too well, even against tyrant old ladies!

# Chapter 8
# Selling an Asset

Let's take a bread-and-butter example involving the sale of a valuable asset such as a factory. You have expanded elsewhere and have no use for the particular factory so you decide to employ an agent to market the property. This will permit you to stand back from direct negotiations out of reach of your opposite number as explained in chapter four.

You are not put to the sword directly and so your opposite number cannot approach you or make deductions about your position other than through the agent. Whether you deal with potential purchasers directly or not is always a carefully balanced but important decision. Of course in the case of selling a factory there are far more complications than merely selling a residential property, but many of the facets remain the same. Negotiations will necessarily be multi-layered.

The availability of good transport links, local footfall and such technical considerations as overhead cranes, location of production runs, ample water supplies, and much besides are all taken into account both when advertising a sale, or when considering a purchase. A common belief with house sales is that agents simply recommend you to lower the price, sometimes at a considerable loss, in order to enhance a sale and gain a result at any cost. I have found that with a good agent he will be capable of negotiating skilfully providing you brief him well and convince him you are no "push-over." He will gain experience of your position as each and every enquiring party comes forward and raises questions, and with your assistance will be well prepared to give the most telling responses relevant to the situation. And so far as price is concerned you can always ask for offers over and above a minimum level as a favourite means of restricting low offers on price.

A party of prospective buyers will arrive to be shown around the facility. They will walk around taking note of the communication and transport needs, layout, power points, electrical and gas services, water inputs, conveniences and offices, building heights and other dimensions and a multitude of other things as they proceed. If you chose to be in their company just about the most commonly employed tactic you can anticipate is that they will, albeit politely, "rubbish" what it is they see. This may be real or invented, but is done in the interests of bargaining the price down. And when there is a firm chance of a sale in prospect the parties meet, shall we say in the boardroom, to discuss the deal.

It may not seem important at this stage but you have to decide who it is you want in your negotiating team, if anybody, or will you be inclined to conduct the whole matter yourself. Surprisingly enough this brings us to an important negotiating principle in itself. Imagine you are facing a well drilled team on the opposite side of the table that impatiently fires loads of questions at you simultaneously. The author suffered this treatment once at a lunch given by a French bank. Whilst each of my hosts ate their meal the others in turn fired their questions, and my meal was getting colder and colder as I was expected to respond!

They may have chosen a significantly large team to rely on the weight of numbers, but we know there are flaws in this approach. You may have detected that some of them are keen on one aspect whilst others not so keen. You will have made a judgement as to what is most important to them, and which party is likely to have the greatest influence on the others. Your advantage is that you may chose not to have colleagues on your side interrupting your words, or deflecting you from your chosen path. You can set one of the opposing party against the other to push the discussion in the direction you want. Or you can do so merely to cause a little mischief and confusion in the ranks in order to take the upper hand yourself.

You will of course have taken independent advice on the value of your factory and considered all the alternatives that you or a third party might put the factory to. You will have assessed its particular locational and other advantages and familiarised yourself with its disadvantages in advance. And now you must pay particular attention to work out exactly what it is that draws your potential purchasers to your factory or other property. Once you know this you can draw attention to the fact your factory may be uniquely appropriate to their requirements. It may even be located somewhere that gives it a particularly high value of which you were hitherto unaware! You will be using professional techniques with which all top negotiators are fully equipped. Every issue you

67

handle with expertise, every pitfall you avoid, will all enhance your position. You will aim at the maximum result to your advantage and feel when agreement is finally reached that the effort and advance preparation has been fully worthwhile.

If the negotiations are sat on a fine line, then you will consider what you can throw in at least cost to yourself that will clinch the deal. This could, for example, be your willingness to vacate the factory a few months early at no extra charge. There may be other actions you can employ to facilitate the ease through which your buyers can set up their operations. You might make space available. You may offer assistance with transport once your own capacity is no longer required. You may throw in your stock of fuel oil and the like which would be difficult to transport in any event. You will consider anything whatever that you feel might tip the scales towards a favourable conclusion. And you will get a good clue as to what might accomplish this end by close observation and attention for the duration of the negotiations.

Let's put ourselves in the position of the potential buyers.

A ploy often used is for that party to bluster and puff and blow, threaten to walk away, and all those other means of dominating in a quasi-threatening manner. They will offer a scandalously low price, saying they can do much better elsewhere. They may contend an alternative deal is all but ready to be struck, ready for their solicitors to complete. They will show impatience if they do not get an immediate answer in their favour. If you hide behind the oft fabled "higher authority" they will throw scorn at you. They will suggest you refer them to the person that has the requisite authority and stop wasting their time. They will no doubt use as many of the tactics we have discussed earlier as they are able to employ. And if they are any good, they will not do so too overtly. A point delivered in a well-reasoned gentle manner is worth ten that involve raised voices and such antics! This is all well worth remembering.

Take care not to be hustled into a quick agreement if you feel you are behind in the race. Don't decide something in haste to regret afterwards. Anticipate bluster and stay calm. Hold your end up and ooze confidence. Call their bluff. There is nothing like suggesting they pursue their "alternative" deal to put paid to a bluff, and then you will have the upper hand. If they were not interested, they wouldn't be there in the first place, so know your bottom line and your goals, and remain cool.

Often viewers will praise everything they see to the heavens and you grow in confidence that a good deal is near certain. Their objective, if only subconsciously, is to build bon homie and trust. So be careful. It comes at a price so when you are still not happy with the proposal they will lean on the goodwill and friendship they feel they have engendered with you. Start feeling guilty now and you are lost! And those that flatter and compliment everything they see as they walk around are strangely enough the most likely to abandon the purchase without trace. A favourite agent I once employed said she called such people "gushers" and advised me to ignore them on first sight! She rightly described them as time wasters! All that "gushing" and you may never hear from them again!

This is basically routine bread and butter stuff, but no two negotiations are ever the same. You will be surprised if you take an analytical approach just how many useful negotiating tactics you will note along the way in your endeavours.

**Key Tactics Summary**
Prepare in advance.
Know your advantages and disadvantages.
Know what your buyers rate most highly.
Spot the spoiling tactics used to undervalue your asset.
Think carefully about the size and content of your team.
Decide whether and when to proceed at arm's length.
Recognise when "competing deals" are genuine or invented.
You may have a ghost "competing deal" of your own.
Know how to combat bluster.
Stay cool, don't resort to aggression or get personal.
Be reasonable if you want a deal.
Consider last minute concessions that can make a deal.
Beware of "gushers"!

# Chapter 9
# Sundry Cases

One of my favourite places to visit on business was Sweden where we had a vibrant business in selling spectacle frames. Luxottica supplied a range of frames that was a very popular product for our company there. Manufacturing took place at Cortina in Italy, quite close to the famous ski centre. We were most concerned to receive an approach from them one day with a view to their purchasing our company with the intention of expanding it further into Scandinavia themselves. They had done their homework and, without our knowledge, had conducted preliminary negotiations with our local management. They in turn were open to accepting the proposal.

We on the other hand didn't want to lose the profits they contributed to our consolidated group accounts. It fell to me to go down to Cortina in the grips of an icy winter to negotiate on behalf of the group. I could barely stand up on the icy roadways so I was clearly never cut out to ski down the slopes that confronted me.

After preliminaries I was finally introduced to the "big man" at the top! I ascribe this title to him because he had an air about him that was ultra-respected by all around. Perhaps "feared" might be a better choice of words. His deep monotone gravelly voice was reminiscent of Marlon Brando in the "Godfather," and it would have been easy to imagine he had connections in that direction. And when they assured me

*"I was okay,"*

that the boss

*"liked me,"*

the message was conveyed in such a way that I should be more than a little bit thankful! So a good start but how do you negotiate with such a man!?

First of all, I congratulated both Luxottica and ourselves on making such a success of the business we were in together. I pointed out it had been a long relationship beneficial to both sides and that it would be a great pity to take any precipitative action that might harm these mutual interests. He was told we would be very reluctant to sell, not least because to do so we would be obliged to manufacture a competing frame ourselves. After all the years of friendship we would end up competing with them! And that was just about the best I could come up with as the die seemed to be well and truly cast.

That we did make gold half eye frames, and had been the major manufacturer of the old-fashioned national health frames years ago stood as testament to the fact we had a frame making facility. That we could manufacture anything that remotely competed with the Luxottica frames was laughable, not that I was about to reveal that fact!

So my negotiation ploy for what it was depended on a degree of flattery, a pinch of bonhomie, an effort to suggest harm would come of such a move, and in the last analysis a friendly hint that amounted to a veiled threat! By the time we shook hands as the meeting concluded I knew I had done enough, at least for now! I duly returned to brief the board at the next meeting. When asked how I had averted what looked like a forced sale, the staff and all on board, I reported I had said in the last resort we would make our own frames. On hearing that one of my more dour colleagues, the one perhaps with the greatest knowledge of frames, nearly fell off his chair. "But we couldn't possibly do that," he snorted, to which I merely replied, "But he doesn't know that!" And that's how it ended up!

Strangely enough I encountered another rather intimidating gentleman whom I also learned "liked me" in Old Ford in Tower Hamlets, London. They were importers of edible nuts. This time we had a common interest since we were both tenants in a property owned by a third party who was trying to steal a march on us. My recommendation was that we pooled our strengths and re-fashioned several aspects of the situation to our mutual advantage. Negotiating together we succeeded when neither one of us would have done so acting alone.

A very unorthodox "negotiation" was once unwittingly conducted by me in a pub with a local farm hand in a rural village where we lived. On realising the video recorder I had recently purchased for recording a trek through Nepal had been superseded by a more practical model, I was bemoaning the fact I bought it in the first place. As if daydreaming, I ventured to say, between downing my beer, that I just wished somebody would break into the house one night without harming anybody or touching anything else, and make off with the unwanted machine. Before I had even collected my senses one night I was woken to some noise. We went downstairs to my horror to see the deed had actually been done! My wishes had been carried out to the letter! My wife had called the police before I made the connection with that calamitous comment in the pub, and they duly turned up to take fingerprints and all else! Not my most noble "negotiation" attempt I must confess. My careless talk had doubtless led to the crime but whoever it was I was chatting with that night had completely escaped my mind. I could hardly identify him if it hadn't! This surely ranked amongst the strangest "negotiations" I can ever recall having shamelessly completed, and I feel guilty to this day!

There was an incident in the commercial catering industry when a customer had been badly scalded because a coffee decanter had collapsed in her hands without notice. We were facing a legal challenge when a glance at the bottom of the decanter told me something was wrong. I couldn't see the traditional identity code, I think DD510 embossed on the bottom by Jobling's of Sunderland, our sub-contract manufacturer. It was as it turned out an identical copy made of inferior materials by a company in Japan. But to whom would we complain? What negotiation or demands were possible at such a distance? The answer was provided by our solicitors and we went along with their advice by agreeing a letter to the Japanese embassy duly composed by them. We received an apology and they kept their word never to place us in jeopardy again.

Our coffee machines were used within the business as part of an office services scheme, but also sold to the Kenco coffee company in very substantial numbers. Between us it was said we were at the forefront of the country's conversion from tea to coffee drinkers. But whilst they were prospering our margins were diminishing, and a meeting had been called by the baronet Sir Geoffrey Vavasour, who managed that side of our business, to discuss prices. He wanted me to attend what really amounted to my first attempt at being a salesman! As a team I thought he and I complemented each other rather well, but for a seaman cum sales and service executive. asking for a price increase didn't come naturally! He was almost too nice and accommodating for that! So I played the villain with my trusty calculator, and Geoffrey the mediator. To understand the point, you will need to consider that very few such sophisticated machines were on the market at that time, and they still held novelty value.

We all sat down to a splendid cup of Kenco coffee. We gave some thought to what it was we could offer Kenco to smooth the way, and we came up with some technical advice they required on the optimum temperature at which water should be ejected onto the coffee beans. This new knowledge we had gleaned from our research and development department. Thus armed, the serious discussions commenced and we had good prospects of each side leaving satisfied, that win-win situation accomplished.

My calculations had shown if you indexed the last agreed price from the date it was fixed to the present day at average inflation rates (x) the price would be (y). And we could afford to look for something lower than that since we had made economies in the machine elsewhere, which fact we kept to ourselves. As my fingers sped over the calculator indexing the price up period by period our hosts could barely keep pace. The result was much higher than the price we were requesting and to resist would have been very difficult for them. I think it might be fair to say they were bamboozled by my calculator and we got our price! After another coffee and some hilarious nautical stories by Geoffrey we parted as always as good friends!

There was a time when the author was engaged in an exercise to rationalise the paperwork used to get products out of the stores and into the sales ledgers at Fort Dunlop.

No less than two "docket sets" were employed as we called them and each piece of paper in each set had to be handled by an employee as part of the overall system. My aim was to log all the movements of bits of paper on what we knew as a "flow chart" and then review the way it worked to see how inefficiencies built into the system could be eradicated. The maxim as always in such operations was that the longer the flow chart resulting, the greater the number of staff you had to employ, and vice versa. When the original flow chart of some five feet was finally reduced to an achievable one of eighteen inches it meant that staff redeployment and redundancy negotiations would follow.

Even acquiring the information as to what each employee did with each piece of paper landing on their desk involved a degree of reluctance, of rebuttal, negotiation and some amusement. Nobody had much of a clue what happened next after they performed their function. Nor did they know what had gone before! A typical response to where a form had come from would be to say it "always arrived on a Tuesday, and was placed by somebody unknown in the in-tray." "It was then processed and taken out again the next day from the out-tray at the end of the desk!" There was no concept of the overall system or even what it was it purported to achieve exactly. Multi mini negotiations along the route were all necessary to make any progress whatever. The discussions could sometimes be tedious but often fun. In the end we got the job done largely by weight of personality in seeking cooperation.

### Key Tactics Summary
Using bluff can be a very valuable tactic.
Join forces with third parties if you have a mutual interest.
A sharp legally constructed letter does more than one on company letter head.
Establish some bon homie at a meeting before you get around to the unpalatable business of the day.
Tell it like it is!
Know the value of being curious and thorough.
Nautical stories always break the ice!

# Chapter 10
# On a Lighter Note

It has already been acknowledged how very little communication between parties can constitute a negotiation. In legal terms a contract requires an offer and an acceptance which will then be complete upon acceptance and delivery. The negotiation is the stage prior to contract. You could say that it is the negotiation phase that matures into a contract, so of its nature it is itself composed of an offer and acceptance in embryo form. In the negotiation stage it will not however have been committed to writing and signed and sealed, and in many cases never will be if it is acted upon and concluded without the need for a written contract.

We have already alluded to the fact that a negotiation can occur in the simplest of ways, not necessarily even involving as much as the spoken word. So it will not surprise you to know that many day-to-day negotiations take place without you hardly noticing they have, and in many cases they will have been negotiated and acted upon more or less instantly. Such instances can be quite entertaining, if not informative. So in this chapter we are going to lighten the subject a little and take a look at a few light-hearted examples. The first involves matters of the heart.

My home was within easy reach of a local beauty spot on top of a hill from which you could see all the lights of industry in all directions. It was a pleasant place to walk dogs during the day, and a haven for romantic couples in the night-time. But if you suggested to a date you should go up to this spot you were in danger of getting a slap across the face, such was its reputation! I had been out on a date with a girlfriend I had known for a while, and it so happened we had to drive past the junction which led up to this haven. As we approached the turn off, I dearly wished I could find the courage and the right words, but doubted they would ever come out without my going red in the face and barely audible.

And then a solution occurred to me! I engaged my indicator as though to turn right and simply looked questionably at her. The nod of approval cemented the deal and I wondered how it could ever have been so simple without as much as a spoken word! What had taken place was a negotiation in every sense of the word as one I might have fumbled unsuccessfully over for weeks and months, if ever! Certainly something to store amongst my negotiating armoury!

We duly arrived to find that night we were the only occupants. However just as passions were running high a patrolling constable appeared and shone a torch right into the car. Actions worked once, I thought, so maybe they would work again! I simply put my side lights on, and he duly went on his way. A second attempt without a word being exchanged! My girlfriend was too far gone it seemed to have the first clue what had happened. What was worse she didn't believe my account when I told her! The moment had passed and now I was feeling nervous about the whole situation. It certainly put an end to our flush of excitement so, my virtue saved yet again, not to mention hers we wound our way home. If I learned anything it was how a simple action like engaging a car indicator spoke volumes in lieu of any spoken negotiation as such. But it wasn't to be a happy ending for I was dismissed a few days later for being totally inept!

Without having any ambition to expand into romantic novels I will relate one more example of a negotiation governed by actions rather than words that I encountered many moons ago! A quick exchange of looks was the opening gambit. As I took large strides at speed along the corridor, I suddenly found her behind me. She was replicating every step without sparing an inch between us. At something of a loss to quite know how to handle the situation I playfully put my hand behind my back, expecting her to retreat fast. Instead, she merely took it and directed it where, had I placed it there myself, I would have most likely been facing her in front of a judge! She refused to let go of my hand until we reached the general office by which time my face was as red as beetroot, my virtue saved once again although not necessarily in my best interests! If only I had been able to oblige her with the key to the board room when she requested it this delicate "negotiation" would have been remembered for all time!

There is much to learn about negotiation surprisingly in the serious game of chess. This war game is by no means the tame boring sport many might imagine. Having to think so hard against the clock more often than not sends your heart rate racing, and at the end of a game it is not uncommon to find yourself almost gasping for breath. The game is rife with tactics and stunts engaged purely to distract and intimidate the opponent. This may start when you offer your hand at the beginning of the game, and your opponent more or less ignores you. They may adopt a smug or hostile attitude to instil fear in your mind. During the game they will intimidate you by banging pieces down to convey, often erroneously but for good effect, their move is fatal to you. In doing so they hope to engender panic and cause you to resign. You may offer a draw and they will forget their manners and play on without saying a word. They might equally vocalise when offered a draw,

*"You must be joking!"*

My opponent once shuffled up and down between moves with hugely distracting squeaky shoes, and when I asked him not to do so he did it all the more!

The end of the game can be even more dramatic. The Cornish chess champion once banged a solid chess board over the head of his opponent. A young opponent that was getting the better of me marked his record sheet up as a "win" for him, and waved it about in front of my eyes to distract me before we had even finished. And the same young hooligan took hold of the clock so I couldn't see my time fast expiring. To stop there and then to appeal to an adjudicator would have disturbed everybody and brought harsh words. The position would have been reviewed and the chances were they would have agreed with him, and would have awarded him the game without further play.

In a national club semi-final against Cheltenham, I've never heard so much noise as when Dr Aitken, a world-famous advocate of the "French Defence" beat our future British champion, and my good friend Owen Hindle. The reigning British champion of enduring fame, Alexander, failed to turn up against Owen for fear he might be risking his grading it was claimed. It was an occasion when numerous international players were present. I was personally paired with Peter Coast. I knew it not at the time but he was the current Scottish champion. "Coast, Peter Coast," he announced himself, sounding for all the world like James Bond in Doctor No! But if that was supposed to intimidate me it was of no effect because, having just been discharged from the Army, I had no idea of the who's who of chess at the time.

Reverting to the fairer sex for one moment in the context of chess the one ploy I am still learning to come to terms with is that little habit some ladies have of deliberately leaning over to reveal a distracting cleavage! And just when you are in deep thought! I'm ashamed to say this distraction has cost me more than one game over my playing career!

The next story involves a different but more romantic insight into the ways of match makers. My sister married a Canadian mounted policeman and moved to Saskatchewan, surrounded by fields of corn for literally hundreds if not thousands of miles. She had never experienced such cold winters and nothing was the same as home, and she desperately missed her home and family. I'm sure more than once the thought would have struck her how much happier things would be if she had family members out there with her. But for my parents this would have been a gigantic step. For myself I was busy qualifying and the notion was furthest from my mind. But then a very plausible reason for joining her was introduced to me on my sister's first trip back home. She was accompanied by a rather lovely friend she had brought along with her, and this lady had already furnished me with one or two ravishing photos such that I was beginning to sense a conspiracy!

I was soon to hear that her father required an accountant for his business in Ontario, and other such overtures. It happens to be a well-worn practice that the first thing accountants who succeed in industry do is to lose the "accountancy" mantle. They are anxious to become known as businessmen, but gaining the title accountant was my prime aim at the time. That said it's best to recognise match making up front as being little more than a devious negotiating method by which lonely people are matched by others who think they know best for them. But if it had been a cunning conspiracy, I would have to admit it very nearly worked!

Negotiating when you are surrounded by guns trained on you by your own army is a very uncomfortable situation to find yourself in! This happened to me during national service when one of the numerous vaccinations they shot into our arms went wrong with a young Welsh soldier. He was removed from the scene hurriedly, being suspected of having contracted the deadly smallpox disease, whilst the rest of us were placed in total isolation. We were told, "Step out of the barrack room and you will be shot on sight," and that was not the kind of negotiation you quarrelled with!

We were surrounded by fully armed soldiers of our own unit on all sides, day and night for around ten days. Volunteers ran over with food and post, and we waited until they were clear away before one of our number would step outside and bring in what they had left. For our part there was no means by which we could contact our families by post or any other method, and the story hit the national press at the time. After some days, a number of us were beginning to feel as though we had untoward symptoms of one kind and another, but they were most likely just imagined rather than real. When it was finally declared our young colleague had been "discharged," whatever that meant, a normally reluctant bunch of young recruits were seen for once running out to the yard to be put through the tough "square bashing" regime in a willing spirit not witnessed ever before!

This next anecdote involves some mechanical help from my trusted calculating machine you will already be familiar with from our Kenco negotiations. It also involves an eighty-five-year-old half Russian half French lady who was still working for the United Nations. I was flying up from one of my regular visits to South Africa and Zimbabwe when I took a stopover at Nairobi to visit the massive gatherings of flamingos to the north. The souvenirs I brought with me from Zimbabwe included a very large picture of elephants carved into a heavy copper base housed in substantial packing. There were two smaller pictures, my general luggage and my video camera. What I hadn't anticipated was all the hotels in Nairobi were fully booked for an African Congress. It was bad enough that the first taxi I hailed couldn't get my luggage into his vehicle, but when I finally stood at the reception of my hotel it was punishing in the extreme to be told there was not a room available anywhere in the city!

This is where that well practiced technique of looking as though you are about to burst into tears can pay off, genuine or otherwise! Luckily one of the young girls behind the desk took pity on me and surrendered her room a day earlier than planned to visit her mother. The next day I checked into the travel agent and met the Russian lady, but we were told there was only one vaguely "L-shaped" room at the hotel. We both declined the offer of a full week in lieu on a safari elsewhere, and decided we would make the best of the situation, but this didn't sit easily with the old lady who was constantly looking unsuccessfully for a way out of the dilemma en route. On little more than a dirt tract we drove over a deadly black mamba that I could see rising up quite visibly through the holes in the foot of the vehicle. A moment later and it would have cleared the holes and fastened itself onto my legs and this account would never have been written!

The jubilant driver stopped the truck and did a victory dance around the remains of this deadly snake. That afternoon on lake Baringa nearly brought its own disaster. This freshwater lake was full of hippos and crocodiles, and unbeknown to me they had negotiated their own mutually satisfying deal. If you approached the hippos too closely, and especially if they had young, they would upend the boat and the crocs would be waiting for a tasty meal! And if that wasn't enough, I had my own problems trying to negotiate with a Dutch lady not to keep standing up and rocking the boat! When we passed a huge hippo, soon afterwards I thought his wide-open mouth represented a smile, but later learned it was a final warning to be ignored at your peril!

The evening was fraught with tension. On returning to the room I found her buried under a mosquito net reading, her spectacles at the end of her nose as she peered suspiciously over them. A grunt from yours truly served as a negotiation I was ready to get undressed for bed, and the lights were dimmed. At four that morning I joined a bird-watching party to view a bird previously declared extinct, but it was the joint effort between a pair of gyr falcons that really took my attention. One struck an already terrified game bird in flight, brought it down to the ground, and started to search for its whereabouts in the undergrowth below. The other remained in the sky signalling instructions as to its location until a piercing shriek signalled the end. It seems that even amongst falcons, dual activities are negotiated to their common advantage! Later that day we saw half a million or so flamingos on the salt lakes, an amazing spectacle if ever there was one, and we made our way back in embarrassed silence to Nairobi.

I will never know how I made it back to the airport with my newly won souvenirs, but at customs control I was met by a most unpleasant individual who fully intended to cause me trouble. He interrogated me about my cash balance, demanding to know how much currency I had brought in or obtained in his country, what I had spent, and what was my balance. Having already anticipated this I was confident it all balanced until it was found I had mislaid just one shilling, and he was acting as though it were a serious crime. He turned his attention to my giant elephant picture, demanding to know what was within the packaging. At the mention of elephants, he went berserk and things were only getting considerably worse!

Now I knew something he didn't! My trusted calculating machine was developing a fault. Apart from using it in the conventional sense you could set it to play "jingle bells" at Christmas, "happy birthday" when appropriate, and so on. But when there was tension in the air the electrics in my own body seem to cause a reaction. The first indication of this would be a "ting" and then moments later it would burst into a rendition of "jingle bells!" I knew well to keep a straight face and make sure my hands were fully on view. And my calculator performed right on cue! Who needs to negotiate when you have such a friend!? My assailant looked suitably terrified as he questioned me and I feigned total ignorance. After another chorus of "jingle bells," it was all too much for him and, in a state of sheer panic he shouted,

*"You go, you go!"*

and I was very happy to oblige! Who would ever have thought a malfunctioning calculator could have saved the day!? But it does show that in a nervous situation, bodily tensions can come to the surface, and I'm sure that some skilled negotiators are capable of picking up on such involuntary signals!

All is to play for and you can be sure that most tradesmen have got a trick or two up their sleeve. Only recently a known contact came around to do one or two jobs. He was accompanied by a "helper" so I immediately anticipated a high charge, since it seemed to me one man was more than adequate for the job. He knew me well enough to turn to his assistant and jokingly hint I had "lots of money." The point of this pseudo "negotiation" was quite clear, and a rather high bill followed as fully anticipated despite my denials!

**Key Tactics Summary**

Learn the non-spoken language of negotiation.

But recognise it when you see it.

Even animals negotiate with each other!

Don't go near the hippos!

Think twice before you cast away your faulty calculator!

Beware match makers!

Take your sunglasses if you play chess!

Turn unexpected situations to your advantage.

# Chapter 11
# The Shake-Up

My first board appointment was to WM Still and Sons Ltd, a family company of nearly a hundred years standing that had been taken over by an international plc when it diversified. For the most part they had been left alone to act as an autonomous entity but had only ever recorded a small profit and were heading for a substantial loss the year I joined. There were many factors explaining why they never recorded a decent profit, including the following.

1. They had let their margins fall by failing to increase prices hoping to win more sales in the north.
2. But they failed to consider the product differences in that vicinity.
3. Neither did they publicise what they were doing.
4. Their product was unnecessarily over-specified.
5. The "empire builder" within their ranks committed more people to his budget year on year, supported by volume expectations that were never realised.
6. The accounts were created city by city rather than by meaningful activities, so the responsible executives for each function had no idea how they were performing.
7. The books of account served the dual purpose of financial and cost accounts, and were so unwieldy the computation of accounts was a nightmare.
8. Coffee machines on hire were too easily "lost" at the end of a contract, neglected or gifted without thought.
9. Maintenance contract prices hadn't been increased for years.
10. Research and Development projects were not prioritised other than by their appeal to the department at their own whim.
11. Value engineering opportunities were spurned.

12. There was little or no control over what the service engineers did with their day. Unresolved issues remained as unpaid debts on the ledgers indefinitely.

In short, as a newcomer, I was facing an enormous task of educating senior management into what I found to be serious shortcomings. Furthermore, there was a massive need for practices to change radically, all of which could never be accomplished without wholesale negotiating with members throughout the organisation. The situation was crying out for a new broom, but by the same token was full of pitfalls wherein individuals fiercely protected their own activities, and would clearly give short shrift to a newcomer to the ranks. I refer to the elements of the task to give the reader the flavour of what had to be negotiated, and to bring the situation I faced to life. At the same time this opportunity gifted me the chance to make my name, you could say. By setting out the management problems, and the means of resolving them, it is hoped that this will be of advantage both in regard to understanding management techniques as well as the prior negotiations without which nothing could have been accomplished.

It was clear at once that this situation was going to require some significant changes both in action and in mindset, and these had to be hard won by persuasive negotiation all the way down the line. But with a managing director who seemed to be getting nowhere it would have been quite remiss had I not seized the opportunity to make my contribution with both hands. My first task, whilst he loomed over me purporting to explain how to prepare a set of accounts (on the back of an envelope) was to completely overhaul the accounts themselves. At the next meeting for the first time, key executives of each function could see how they had performed.

A budget going forward was prepared, the hardest task being to arrest the antics of the "empire builder." There is a common attitude to budgets in many organisations that they are merely "agreed." This is often furthest from the truth, and with "empire builders" they will twist and turn all ways to win their case. Take an overhead out and it will reappear elsewhere under a different guise, and as the new face on the block established management can be intimidating. Such budgets are never merely "agreed" if that denotes a walkover but flat out "hard negotiated!" I knew that very tough negotiations were the only way to make any progress, and I would get no further in my effort until that particular battle was won! Only then would others fall in line and progress could be made under the approving attention of the frustrated managing director. That battle finally won, I felt I was getting somewhere. So my advice would be to recognise what is likely to be your toughest negotiating challenge at the commencement, and tackle it up front whilst you still have the kudos and support to do so.

Putting up prices for the main products was won through arguing common sense, and the marketing strategy up north was all but abandoned for the moment. No reliance was placed on any unobtainable increase in sales, and costs were realigned to match. A single component in the coffee machines was replaced as a first priority by a cheaper component which made a massive difference to the profits it yielded, and with minimum effort.

Projects in the research and development department were listed and reviewed. Only those with high potential to increase profitability were continued. Those that were so continued were ranked in priority order by anticipated results. These were evaluated using discounted cash flow analysis, not previously encountered by the company. It took little negotiation to convince the service department executive to raise his prices substantially on spares and casual repairs. And a major price increase was applied to annual maintenance contracts for the first time in years. Better controls were installed to limit time lost by the service engineers who were otherwise unaccountable for their actions, and commonly went home after completing a single job. A brake was put on the ongoing loss of coffee machines at the end of hire contracts.

The managing director's wife expressed gratitude that her husband was restored to good health, and his habit of referring to me when decisions were required often brought a gathering of directors to my door looking to short circuit the decision-making process. The initial hard-fought negotiations with my peers had been satisfactorily concluded, and the company was in much better shape. We went on to double our profits year on year for six years until we were eventually the greatest provider of profit in the group! No one mocked us any more as the "also ran" business nobody cared about!

With the erosion of time, I encountered salesmen who promised to sell more if only they could grant higher discounts. So I designed a form which they could complete for themselves to justify their suggestion, but never had any takers! Couldn't have been an easier negotiation, that one!

Many management decisions commonly get an airing over a friendly lunch in the local pub. It was there I recall one day, as we were entering our country hideaway, the managing director and the works director were heard hatching some hair brained scheme I instinctively knew would spell disaster. My friend and colleague Sir Geoffrey Vavasour followed me in. He had come down, he said in his cultured "John Hurt" voice,

*"to see his country cousins!"*

He actually looked like John Hurt as it happened and his presence was always felt when he was around. He had been the commander of our once finest battleship, the "Eagle Aircraft Carrier." He was voted the joint greatest amateur sportsman of all time in a competition run by the Sunday Times. Besides which he had the sole right to ride a horse up York Minster, built by his ancestors a thousand years ago. He still had something of the navy about him, and it was he who spotted my hunched-up shoulders, even before I was aware of it myself!

As we entered the Two Sawyers he was heard to comment loudly,

*"If the financial director's back is anything to go by, he is against whatever you two are plotting!"*

To which the managing director responded,

*"Yes, I saw his ears swivel around like an elephant on heat!"*

Geoffrey's laughter rang around the pub, but whatever the crazy idea was we never heard anything more. Just goes to show how even an involuntary hunched up back serves as a negotiating tool!

**Key Tactics Summary**

Stick to your task, be methodical and know your purpose.

Be ready to tackle sacred cows and fixed positions.

A natural reflex reaction can speak volumes.

Well respected colleagues are a great asset.

Don't expect to negotiate miracles.

# Chapter 12
# Roadblocks

There is nothing worse when negotiating if you have to first overcome vested interests. The following will give a few examples of how they might arise. Some might involve skulduggery and self-interest at your expense.

One such experience was in another review of various procedures at Fort Dunlop, Birmingham. The task in hand was to review charges rendered by haulage companies. When I duly arrived at the North Deck, a daunting place, I found it to be full of rubbish, dirt, and a dangerous mix of latex and carbon black everywhere. Rubbish was brought here to be separated between good valuable raw rubber material, to be recycled, and rubbish to be taken by independent haulers to a tip. This was once overseen by a controller on the North Deck but a work study exercise had determined this unnecessary, and the post discontinued. Instead, it would be left to shop personnel to take it to the location and direct it as intended. That is to say good material would be placed in a lift to be sent up to a specialist team who would be working with plant and machinery at their disposal to redirect it back into production, and rubbish would be directed out to a pick-up point for the haulers.

A long line of carriers couldn't wait to fill their lorries fast enough with whatever lay around, and more or less totally without supervision of any kind. Very often they left with their trucks barely half full and nobody took the slightest notice. The costs involved the loss of valuable raw material brought all the way from Malaya, unnecessary haulage costs at inflated rates, unsupervised loads, an idle team responsible for redirecting the good material, and idle recycling plant and machinery. The unemployed recycling team played cards out of sight all day, and they even had a bed tucked away in a corner.

I evaluated the total cost to run into millions and submitted my report to my manager. He had been "promoted sideways" as they say for some misdemeanour in the past and his career progress halted. But it was my report, rewritten under his name, that finally earned him promotion out of the department and his reinstatement! By dressing my report up as his own, and taking full credit for it, he had successfully negotiated his way out of a dead-end position. Whilst the exercise had added much to my confidence, I never got a mention. You learn these lessons it seemed to me the hard way! Of course my career with Dunlop hadn't of itself entered a roadblock, but progress could have been accelerated given fair treatment at the time. As it was, I was fully engaged in mastering the tools of my profession and was already looking for my next move once the position at Fort Dunlop had nothing further to offer me.

Whilst in the machine tool industry a new incentive of investment grants was announced by the government.

The rules were by no means clear and it was my proudest moment that I negotiated a set of clarifying rules at director level at the board of Trade which were to be adopted by the department for use throughout the country. What ranked as consumables, as opposed to medium- or long-term equipment, was a good example of where we had to find a dividing line.

Later a meeting was called between ourselves and the board of Trade to decide exactly what would qualify for the higher level of grants for what could be regarded as "new inventions." At that time, we had developed what we knew as a "Batchmatic" machine which was computer controlled and multi-purpose, at the time a first for the industry. The meeting was called to decide whether our machine ranked as a new invention or simply the adaptation of existing technology. You could argue that all inventions go back to basics such as the invention of the wheel, or the first iron blanks if you see the point, in which event no new invention was ever going to be worthy of the name. So distinctions had to be made, and rules drawn up.

Flushed with a visit from the board of trade, my finance director pushed himself to the fore leaving me completely out of the negotiations. But when the board of trade director refused to continue without my presence, he came in to collect me, more than a little flustered and red in the face! I had already negotiated my way into the goodwill of the board of trade through my actions, and nothing more was required to ensure my involvement in what then transpired. Had this not been the case I would have been facing one of those "roadblocks" we should all be wary of.

You could say I negotiated my way into a job offer during the audit of a company making trailers pulled behind cars. I did no more than suggest he might want to advertise in a sector that hadn't occurred to him, and a job offer resulted.

Not a negotiation in its fullest sense, but my application to the subject certainly eased the path.

It was in the machine tool industry that my company had dismissed an executive who wouldn't go quietly. He was threatening wrongful dismissal, and would arrive each day to his office with little or nothing to do. One Monday morning he was making his way there only to discover what was once his office no longer existed! His office had become a void space integrated into the general office! A team had been called in to what you might consider to be the most violent form of negotiation to which he had no answer, and he left defeated!

**Key Tactics Summary**
Beware lest others steal your negotiated accomplishments.
See beyond the obvious.
Challenge the status quo.
A helpful hint can serve as a pseudo negotiation.
Know that some "negotiations" can be brutal.

# Chapter 13
# In the High Court

The author enjoyed the benefit of an apartment in a converted hotel on the Cornish coast, financed by letting it out to holiday makers in the summer. No other owners let their apartments out. That the author did so was a bone of contention amongst the others. So much so that the chair of the management company, we will call him Manning, tried every conceivable way of encouraging the author to sell up and move out.

A common problem throughout the town was the menace of seagulls who would rip open rubbish bags placed down the front for weekly collection. This resulted in a mess and a potential hazard. So at the first sign of a biscuit wrapper, for example, an attempt was made to take the author to task. All the owners claimed they took their rubbish home for disposal, so there was no chance, they argued, they could ever be the "guilty" party. That when they variously lived at distances of anything up to a hundred or more miles was hard to swallow!

The author liaised with the local council to find a solution to the problem many times, and each time he and the council agreed a course of action the chair encouraged all and sundry to reject the proposal. His aim was clear. The more he could frustrate honest attempts to solve what was a general problem in the area, the more he hoped we would be driven out. He further cemented his position by making himself available to all and sundry to negotiate favours of one kind and another with little or no resistance, so just about everybody was ingratiated to him. And at meetings he acted as "cheerleader" for any mischief or rebel rousing he could cause at my expense. He adopted an air as though he were running a major corporation instead of a small block of apartments, and the atmosphere created was nauseating!

Efforts to successfully convey agreements reached with the Council over rubbish were consistently rejected for reasons beyond credulity. And then at one such meeting the council's advice to place a tarpaulin over the rubbish the night before collection was rejected out of sight. The elderly resident woman from one apartment was the most vociferous against my proposal. Her reason for arguing against it was no more credible than arguing a badger could crawl under the tarpaulin!

At the same meeting I called the chair out for constantly moving our insurance policy. He was an insurance broker and I raised the question of who had benefitted from the commission on the transaction. His claim he had ploughed it back for the benefit of the company was applauded by the others, no evidence of such a claim ever being presented. And the policy was moved around far too often for comfort. Anticipating I would have something to say he adopted a very amateur ploy by insisting I took the seat plumb in the centre of a carefully calibrated semicircle. It was clear his intention was that I would be pilloried by all and sundry in the line of fire sitting around me, but he didn't reckon for my versatility in handling such situations. By placing me in this position he merely gave me the chance to play one against the other, and to expose all of the disarray and contradictions between them! His tactic was a complete failure and I prevailed!

Then, just three weeks after the elderly lady raised the question of the phantom badger, she tripped on something coming down her steps and was seemingly badly injured.

At the least she must have made enough fuss to convey that her very life was in danger because she was air lifted out and taken directly to hospital. When asked what she had tripped on she responded she "wouldn't have tripped on it had she seen it!" The record shows she might come to regret this later!

Needless to say, Manning sprang into action and convinced all and present it must all have been attributable to my paying guests. As a broker himself he immediately contacted the company insurers to lodge a public liability claim, at the same time pointing his finger at me as the guilty party.

That alone precluded me from using the company insurers but by the grace of God I had public liability cover in my contents policy, and pleaded with my insurers not to settle on a "knock for knock" basis. But Manning wasn't done yet. He convinced the old lady she should take me to court, and offered himself as a hostile witness against me!

A guilty verdict in favour of the old lady could potentially have left me in a very poor financial state, even bankrupted me, and he clearly relished the thought! And now I had to wait on tenterhooks for four years for the case to come before the high court in Truro.

The one thing I got absolutely right was to leave a paper trail of all the arguments and discussions we had surrounding the matter, and I commend this always as a vital habit one should adopt. Once the case was announced I knew then that all the minutes and paperwork surrounding the matter would have to be "discovered" by the court, and I took great pains to make sure it was all complete as it would now take the form of evidence.


As the day in court grew closer Manning obtained sworn affidavits from each owner via a solicitor that they were not present on the day of the accident. They willingly perjured themselves as confirmed by my visitors on the day subsequent to the trial, and they each signed their sworn statements.

No evidence as yet had been presented to support any of their claims. I hadn't believed for one moment my visitors were the only ones present in the block on the day, any more than I believed they all took their rubbish home with them at the end of a stay. No evidence had been produced to prove my visitors had in fact in any way been guilty, but of course at this stage the subject was *sub judice*. Everything was by way of presumption along the well-worn path Manning had installed in the minds of the others.

At last, the day of the trial arrived and I duly presented myself. First thing I countenanced was the sight of Manning and his wife sitting smugly, lower down but close to the area occupied by the judge. The old lady didn't appear to have anybody else supporting her. I had been cautioned by my advisors that as an old lady the court was bound to have greater sympathy for her than myself. I was therefore in no way to give any smart answers. I was advised, strongly requested would be more accurate, to keep all my responses short and confined in the main to "yes" and "no" responses! It seemed my hands were well and truly tied behind my back!

# The Language of the Courtroom

The various lawyers arrived sporting their formal wigs, and we all stood for the judge. On my first appearance before a high court, it was all very daunting. The entire process was itself a multi layered negotiation at the highest level. Both sides did nothing less than negotiate with the facts and with the truth, as any layman would interpret the proceedings. One side would take the same facts and attribute one meaning to them, and the other the opposite. The negotiations most often came down to the simple matter of interpretation, but I never thought I would hear myself saying even hard facts can be negotiated! Interpretation is all important, and different versions can be argued starting from the same basis. Those present were negotiating with the party that would decide the issue, whether that be a judge or a jury. It's easy to think that in a courtroom the facts are forensically examined under oath, and the answer speaks for itself. It would be easy to suggest that there is no place in a courtroom for negotiation, that you can't negotiate hard facts, but my eyes were opened.

There is also a great deal of acting goes on. Lawyers cross examining witnesses will want to put on a show.

I was to learn that the officers in such a court all speak and enact a language hitherto unknown to me! I couldn't help but notice the way they would pause in the middle of an interrogation, look up at the ceiling as though having intellectual thoughts out of this world, clear their throats and then continue for effect. And when they were inhibited from speaking, they made good use of facial expressions and body movements into the bargain! Clearly, it was not just going to be about what you said, but how you said it! Anticipation would again be of the utmost importance, and it was likely I would be needing all the tactics I could call for at my disposal. We all see cases in television programmers, if we have not otherwise had the direct experience of appearing in a court, but the strange nature of it all only really hits you I think when you are standing there as I was as the "accused!" It was all theatre of the highest order, and I would soon have my part to play!

## The Key Witnesses

Manning was the first to be addressed and was eager to agree with the judge that we had a problem with refuse disposal. His enthusiasm went up a notch when the judge suggested to him he didn't get on well with yours truly, and he wholeheartedly agreed. His exact words were

*"You could say so, your honour,"*

spoken with great emphasis as though he had scored an important point. But his jaw dropped when the judge made the astute remark that that didn't make me guilty. The papers discovered by the court would have contained a letter from Manning purporting to say he did all the work whilst I sat comfortably at home on my posterior. Again the judge drew attention to the fact that I did attend meetings and I did contribute to the management. Manning retreated to his seat looking somewhat bruised!

Next up came Mrs. Selman, the injured party. She was asked what it was she had tripped over. This time around she gave a very detailed account of anything she could think of, banana skins included! A big mistake!

No mention was made of the vegetation thrown onto her pathway by her other neighbour. It was the case that even when the court case was pending, she had no hesitation in asking me to go around to her property, on her behalf, to wage war on the woman in the next building who was throwing weeds down to her pathway! These could easily have been carried down to the point where she fell, but more to the point how could any normal human being beg favours of another she is about to sue in the high court!? And my advisors, to my surprise and disappointment, refused to make any mention of the unruly dog she was seen handling at the top of the steps that day. Now, four years later, she was able to claim the dog to be well behaved and calm, but that was now and not then!

Despite my briefing my lawyers declined to pick up on the point.

Next the judge took a very astute line of questioning.

*"Which way did you fall?"*

he asked.

*"Could you show me please?"*

leaving it to the advocate to demonstrate on behalf of the plaintiff.

Of course it's far easier to fall backwards if you slip on something than forwards, and that would have carried her even further away from the area our rubbish could possibly have reached. Then we had the amusing spectacle of the

Prosecuting Lawyer trying to demonstrate how she might have fallen, and correcting his fall halfway through when he realised he had been duped!

## My Turn in the Box

It finally got around to my turn to appear in the witness box and be sworn in. Now I knew I would have to be in full negotiating mode. My adversary hurled a barrage of abuse and innuendo at me. After a number of exchanges, he was ready to put me to the sword.

*"Is it not true that a seagull could have strewn the contents of a bag over the area and the woman had slipped on them causing herself such injury?*

*Couldn't such a seagull have picked up a scrap of food, dropped it two or three steps higher, and then left it upon being startled at exactly the position Mrs. Selman tripped upon?*

*Was this not the case?"*

he impatiently demanded to know!

The instructions I had been given echoed in my ears, but how could I have simply said "yes!" In theory it was undeniable that, however unlikely given the lie of the land, it could always have happened as he suggested. But a simple "yes" would surely be taken as an admittance of guilt with all the consequences that would bring, both financially and in the eyes of Manning and company! I determined not to be browbeaten into what I could and couldn't say.

That was never going to do!

## Saved by the Seagull

I continued,

*"Your Honour, I've been interested in bird life for many years, and have watched how seagulls behave if they should be disturbed when scavenging for food many times."*

I found myself getting into the theatrical mood I had been observing thus far all morning. So I paused, made the compulsory stare at the ceiling as though gathering very profound thoughts, cleared my throat, and continued…

*"But in those circumstances,"*

I continued,

*"they usually fly out to sea with their scraps rather than surrender them."*

A longer pause…

94

*"I have never seen one fly directly at a brick wall, around a corner, and up a flight of stairs."*

Pause…

*"Your Honour…"*

At this point my attorney put aside the advice he had handed out and made a very demonstrable show of "silent laughing." His shoulders heaved up and down as though to emphasise the point, but no noise came out of his mouth. Dutifully the rest of his colleagues followed his antics! I felt I was now entering sitcom territory! Clearly the intention was to attract the judge's attention and underscore my own delivery. It was certainly theatrical and becoming ever more so as matters progressed. In supporting my own words in this manner, they were of themselves clearly adding to the weight of the "negotiation" attempting to win the judge's mind and influence the outcome.

Of course that didn't please the prosecuting advocate one bit, and not least because the judge could barely mask the utter amusement on his face! He now tore into me in an ill temper which I'm sure did him no good at all.

*"Very funny,"*

he snapped. So he tried a different angle.

*"If not seagulls, what about cats?"*

Then he abandoned cats, having seen the weakness in his own argument, if you have ever tried to take anything off a cat. He finally put all his hopes on a mighty wind that would have blown food around the corner and up two or three steps. I adopted a more conciliatory mode and agreed this might be possible, adding it would take something like a typhoon to obtain that effect. By now the prosecuting lawyer was looking very dishevelled as a result of his own antics. I felt victory was perhaps even in sight!

The judge recovered from his struggle to keep a straight face and prompted me in his own right to answer some further questions. I was able to explain just how much I had liaised with the authorities in a serious effort to find a solution to the problem. I was able to repeat the story of the badger to which he incredulously questioned,

*"A badger!?"*

as though the world had gone mad!

*"Yes, a badger, Your Honour,"*

I responded and it hit home!

## My Witnesses

My guests from the week prior to the accident had received subpoenas to attend all the way from the north-east, as were the couple who occupied the apartment the week before from Suffolk. They first swore they were there at the material time, and there was no such rubbish. They had been holidaying as a foursome for twenty years and each day one or other of them would dispose of their rubbish elsewhere and that was their established custom. They were to confirm to me subsequently that, despite signing affidavits, a number of owners were indeed present in the premises on the unfortunate day of the accident! The next witnesses to be called explained they both had a serious allergy to bananas! Had they eaten any then both of them would have ended up in hospital! How such a couple ever became acquainted is something I've wondered about ever since, most likely receiving treatment for the allergy perhaps at the same time!

## The Verdict

The judge eventually retired to consider his verdict and returned to tell the old lady she had received rather bad advice! Of course the main person advising her was Manning! I was exonerated whilst the other side had to pay the costs. Manning headed immediately out of the courtroom, shaking, broken and reddened with high blood pressure and anger, and trying as much as possible to make himself invisible. He left the old lady he had served so dishonourably to her own devices, not that I could find it in my heart to feel much sympathy for her!

## Manning

What of Manning!? He swore he never wanted to be seen in my company ever again! The insurers informed me they had blacklisted him for nefarious business operations, and his accounts told a sorry story. The next day he put his apartment on the market, and I never cast eyes on him ever again! What started with a concerted effort on his part to drive us out of our apartment concluded with he himself being the one to go!

Over the years people sold and bought the apartments and today the story has changed radically. We are now in the minority of those that do not let their apartments out. Manning's cultivated followers, or at least those that remained, changed their tune and peace was restored. One of Manning's greatest supporters, the one that proposed the surcharge on my service charges, was heard to declare,

*"He would sooner stand with me than in front of me!"*

The old lady died a few years later and nobody has tripped down the steps since! The battle was over and won and the battle scars long since healed.

I'm sure that there must be many such cases when residents in blocks of apartments resent individuals letting theirs out for profit. Perhaps my struggle with such an event might lay down a blueprint for action for others that follow!

**Key Tactics Summary**

The meeting called to interrogate me was a good example of "one versus the rest" and how best to deal with it.

Giving the seat of honour to somebody can be a two-edged sword!

So divide and rule.

Grind out a win however long it takes.

Know your rights and know how to defend them.

Always leave a paper trail.

Remember that quaint court language. Do gaze at the ceiling, pause, clear your throat and carry on! If nothing else it will make you feel good!

In a court, negotiating skills are as important as ever.

Use humour without overtly showing it.

Remember seagulls can make excellent witnesses.

# Chapter 14
# The Chat in the Urinals

Of all the ways to commence a negotiation, you might think a casual remark in the urinals might be rather innocuous, but that in this story eventually killed off an entirely successful British industry, and quite unnecessarily so!

Few business transactions come more complex or of greater significance than takeover negotiations, and this one went first to the Office of Fair Trading and was then referred to the Monopolies Commission, which was later reinvented as the Competition Commission.

My group were the largest manufacturer of glass ophthalmic lenses in the world, churning out millions upon millions at cheap prices to supply the retail industry giving enhanced sight to millions of people. It also gave work to over six thousand persons, and it was a good feeling to be working in such a philanthropic atmosphere. There was an interim stage between ourselves as mass manufacturers and the retail end of the market, and this was known as the prescription houses, of which we owned some twenty per cent. We made frames, but very few.

The group managing director and chief executive, Sir Ian Morrow, has been referred to earlier. I would describe him more as a fire fighter than a planner, but he was very shrewd and didn't miss many opportunities. He always said his most fruitful negotiations came when he consulted the shop floor over a problem, as they knew best what was going on! He told me once that, had his father not retired at the age of eighty-seven, he would have made it to a hundred. And there was no way he was going to retire "prematurely" which should have been a clue he was going to stick around for some time!

I recall one day chatting with him in the boardroom after a meeting called to determine our response to threatened strike action. The strikers weren't altogether very well informed, as I witnessed at first hand when driving into work one morning. The pickets were exhibiting placards saying,

*"If you can spend all this money on depreciation, what about the workers?"*

Depreciation being just a book entry of course they had picked up from the accounts! As we stood there chatting Ian spotted a worker hanging around the boardroom door seemingly fixing something or other. Sharp as a needle Ian turned to me with that particular look on his face which conveyed so much, and said,

*"John, at the first sign of any go-slow or nonsense suspend the lot immediately!"*

He knew what the fellow was about and equally well knew that the message would be carried back forthwith to the militant plating shop! A rather neat piece of negotiation and I had to take my hat off to him!

We bought our glass blanks from Pilkington in a harmonious relationship that stretched back many years.

At Christmas time Ian was invited to the Pilkington Christmas dinner as was the custom. Pilkington were at the time very aggressive in the take-over market. The word was that without exception they always got their target. I knew from the smug look on Ian's face when he came in the next morning he had been up to some mischief or other! It didn't take him long to boast he had had a "very interesting chat" with Alastair Pilkington as they stood side by side in the urinals!

The conversation went as follows. First Ian:

*"I see you have been very busy with acquisitions lately Alastair!"*

Then Alastair:

*"Yes, we're always on the lookout!"*

And Ian:

*"I'm surprised you have never looked in our direction!"*

Ian knew well what he was doing, and he was playing Russian roulette. I just scowled at him as he related the incident. For me running the company successfully was all important. For Ian, who had literally hundreds of directorships, he saw companies come and go all the time. Moreover, when he offloaded a company, the chances were he would make it a condition he joined the board of the acquiring company as part of the deal. Having remained loyal to us for a great many years this latest development surprised as much as disappointed me, and he mentioned not what would happen to my position if his little bit of mischief came to fruition.

This resulted in an invitation for Ian and John Wiseman to go up to St Helens to discuss the possibility of an agreed take-over. John was a very fiery individual who won high accolades in the war for escapades such as throwing himself on a grenade to save his men. As it was the grenade never exploded but he was not to know that. He also got imprisoned by the enemy, escaped, and joined the French Resistance causing mayhem. He once mounted a machine gun to the front of a motor cycle, chose a flat exposed stretch of railway line where the enemy troop trains would pass, and as he sped the length of the carriages took out scores if not hundreds of the enemy before making his getaway. He was finally injured and shipped back home highly decorated to head up the SAS head office in the south of England.

The discussions at St Helens were productive and they even agreed the price at which shares would change hands! That is until John mentioned in passing that, of course he and Ian would join the Pilkington Board! When that didn't go down well John suggested that at least Ian should be on their board, and that failed just as badly. On that revelation both Ian and John stormed out of the meeting! But they had whetted Alastair's appetite and annoyed him into the bargain. The very next day Pilkington made a bid for the company over their heads directly to the shareholders. And they did so at a lower price than that they had all cheerfully agreed the day before at St Helens. That price was going to be a weight around Ian's neck for years to come!

Thanks to Ian's tacit comment in the urinals I, along with others, would now be working our socks off to the small hours defending our very independence. This would last at least a year whilst both sides put their whole into defending their entrenched positions. Worse the business itself would suffer through the distraction of it all, and the reverberations would be with us for years to come! Like throwing a pebble into the pond the matter would not be concluded by the outcome of the Pilkington bid alone. Now nothing would ever be the same again! It goes to prove that negotiating by seemingly innocent little side remarks can lead off in all directions, some desirable others not so!

The follow up negotiations would all now go up a notch or two. Written statements would be dispatched to our shareholders explaining our position for resisting a takeover. At one moment we would have been advocating the takeover, but now all our publicity advised quite the opposite. Meetings with shareholders and advisory experts in our merchant bank and elsewhere would follow. As things progressed that reference would be made to the Office of Fair Trading and then to the Monopolies, or Competition Commission.

The first requirement of any disputed take over is to build up a list of your defences. Some are traditional negotiating actions in the circumstances such as producing encouraging profit forecasts, and committing a higher dividend to keep the shareholders on side. You would also give an indication of your future growth prospects, and highlight any negative aspects of the proposed takeover that would harm the company. Appearing in front of the commission we would certainly be making the point that the proposal would create a substantial vertical integration from the first blanks to the finished spectacles. This is a very complex matter and we are now entering some big-time negotiating scenarios.

Our defence schedule would have appeared as follows.

1. An attractive profit forecast.
2. A dividend commitment.
3. Comparative trends in earnings per share.
4. Business outlook.
5. Forward prospects.
6. Any exciting projects or developments in the pipeline.
7. Flaws foreseen in the aggressor.
8. Lack of experience in the aggressor.
9. Outright misconceptions and risks in the aggressor.
10. The disservice to the public of such a large monopoly.
11. And whatever else it was thought might be useful.

When it came in due course to the hearing at the Commission, we had to employ the most expensive top barristers and other legal advisors. We would be arguing the case on multiple levels, and would have to be so prepared the demands of the business would take second place for some time. At the time preparation of accounts by reference to inflation accounting was a new fad, so accounts prepared by traditional means had to be recalculated for each company and compared as an indicator of efficiency for the past five years side by side. We had to find as many ways as possible to convince shareholders we were the more efficient and their returns stood to be better by showing us loyalty. The burden of it all was enormous, and it was Pilkington who would have the advantage because they were far more preoccupied with acquisitions than ourselves. As mentioned, they had a reputation for never failing to get their quarry!

Finally, the day of the hearing before the commission arrived. It was chaired by Sir Roger Falk and our lead barrister was Sir Jeremy Lever. We lined up with Sir Ian and other key notables from our management together with our chairman, D'Arcy Biss. D'Arcy opened our case very eloquently and asked that all further questions be directed to Sir Ian. Right at the beginning it was obvious the commission had caught wind of the "chance remark" as it was called in the urinals. Why, we were asked, if you were touting a takeover then can you now say you are opposed to it? My heart sank and I had no idea how we might recover from that opening question. But it seemed Alastair, perhaps for some question of honour, didn't want to make a big issue out of the matter. Perhaps what transpired at St Helens would have embarrassed him. Ian "thought he could remember the chat" but they were "all celebrating at a Christmas party" so, "if he had said it, it didn't mean anything!" I could hardly believe my ears but the moment passed and the questions continued hard and fast.

There was much debate on which company had the greater technical expertise, how Pilkington could do so much better if they had full control over the processes, how on the other hand they were continually letting us down on service and new developments and so on. The debate got ever deeper into minute technological detail that our experts handled very well. Pilkington, we said, were not developing the right glass for our needs. We had communicated this to them many times. Should an acquisition be permitted there would be no pressure on them to do so into the future. And we rebutted their contention they needed to own us to understand our requirements because they had themselves already taken over a major prescription house, so should already be fully informed. I couldn't quite see the relevance since a prescription house was not the same as us, but the moment again passed.

An expert recruiting firm had been drafted in by us to report how happy our management were, as though anybody would be prepared to say anything to the contrary! Then we were "gifted" a line of argument that would make Pilkington look rather foolish! Post-acquisition it was revealed they planned to move a substantial part of the manufacture to South Africa. The usual reason for such a plan was to take advantage of cheaper labour, there being no obvious distribution benefit. But from our experience such operations require a more substantial home market to support the operation. Others had tried and had failed.

Attention was drawn to our lack of young executive appointees to follow in the footsteps of Ian, and we were indeed scant on the ground. In fact, I was the only one in the room that Ian could point to as an example for the future, and that was a moot point considering how much power he garnered to himself! Not to mention he had already expressed his intentions of staying around for a very long time! The record will show that he was still at the helm of a good few companies even at the age of ninety as reported by the Sunday Times in due course!

The debate continued day after day until the commission finally exhausted all their questions. Sir Jeremy Lever QC was invited to summarise our position. What followed was entertainment of the highest order. From the questions we were asked, and from the scraps of information we picked up we began to get a fair idea of what the Pilkington plans would be should their bid succeed. Many of these seemed impractical and damaging given our intimate knowledge of the industry, not the least the notion of moving production to South Africa. Sir Jeremy suggested to the commission he would like to take the assumed role of a fly on the wall listening in to the Pilkington directors discussing the bid. What followed was the most amusing summing up one can imagine. It was full of mockery, derision and satire. One by one the imaginary Pilkington directors were asked for their input, and in each case they either gave hopelessly wrong answers, didn't have an answer at all, or promised to go and find out. And each time what was proposed was knocked down in this brilliant sketch. At one point the invented conversation had the production facility located in the poverty-stricken township of Soweto on the outskirts of Johannesburg, and I seem to remember something of that kind actually being tossed at us by the commission.

Having finished his parody the commission acknowledged it, but said they would not be unduly influenced by his undoubted acting ability. They did however say it gave them the assurance that should he ever be out of a job then an acting career awaited him!

Finally came the announcement we had won. We now had to revert to running the company properly, so much of our time having been deflected for so long. We were now bearing serious scars. We would have to "scrape the barrel" to meet the profits forecast, and release the cash to meet the higher dividend commitment. Serious aspects of the business had been neglected. Nothing was ever going to be the same again!

All for that sly comment in the urinals!

**Key Tactics Summary**
Note the method of "opportunity negotiating" used in the doorway of the boardroom during the strike.
Note well the power of the negotiation by innuendo.
Never do anything to invite an unwanted takeover bid.
In a hostile bid first prepare an exhaustive defence list.
Beware casual chats in the loo or any place else can have disastrous consequences.

# Chapter 15
# The Russian Job

Back at our Head Office in Mill Hill we benefitted from what might be regarded at the time as a monopoly in supplying Russia for some time with its need for lenses. Their purchase order came to millions of pounds worth in one single composite order, containing lenses of each and every shape, size and variation throughout the entire range. I doubt that any other company could have handled such an order in a single transaction. Payment was arranged in Indian rupees of which Russia had a surplus at the time, and so multi-currency transactions were involved before we received the sterling value in the UK.

This wasn't the only area where pitfalls abounded. We had to take great pains to acquire a certain knowledge of the paperwork that had to be completed. It was not unknown for consignments to be shipped to Russia and for the paperwork to be challenged for errors on arrival. This would result in the order being cancelled by default. We had heard of such instances when the goods could not be recovered so Russia got them for nothing, and organisations never redeemed their worth! The word was that Russia was working the system for exactly that reason. A team would pour over all and any documents and procedures, and if they should find fault, they were not beyond using the discrepancies to their own advantage!

So I and a colleague with more experience than I in shipping documentation took ourselves off to the local branch of the Russian bank based in London. Our purpose was to hear it directly from "the horse's mouth" you could say that there were no flaws of any kind in the paperwork we had prepared. This would be a most essential but cautious piece of negotiating in the circumstances. On their assurances we gave the signal for the trucks to leave and the long journey overland commenced. An enormous value in the shape of lenses would now thread its way through numerous countries until it finally reached its destination.

The transaction proved to be successful and our monies were duly received in our own bank as expected. My colleague and I breathed again!

The Russians tended to embark on this kind of huge transaction from time to time when they had enough currency at their disposal, and such transactions in various products were not so unusual. So when we quoted for another such consignment a year later, we were more than a little confidant we would get the order. But no order followed.

It was finally announced a company with the unlikely name of "Flingmay" had secured the order. But how could they possibly have done so since they themselves didn't manufacture a single lens!? The answer lies with one very enterprising individual whose name escapes me, but his scheme was quite outrageous! He first of all offered to quote, and so was handed the breath-taking schedule of quantities by lens type and quantity. He then visited multiple sources of lenses around the world, and set up provisional orders with each and every one of them according to whichever lenses they were capable of supplying. No doubt some difficult products might even have been our own, obtained indirectly. By fair means or foul, he cobbled together enough lenses from multi sources to meet the order. His price for the entirety beat ours and, incredibly, the Russians put their trust in him and the order was duly completed!

This must have involved negotiations on a scale never encountered in the industry before. He must have had an air of confidence and abilities that impressed the hard-nosed Russians unless he resorted to tactics of which we can only wonder.

One day, in another capacity, I finally met up with the said gentleman. Forewarned of what was likely to happen I shirked doing any business with him as I considered the risks to be too high. But I did get the smallest clue to how he might have impressed people so effectively. I received a little goodwill incentive in the form of a Chinese painting of no particular value, which hung in my bathroom for a few years! I asked myself was that all it took to woo Russia!? Who knows, maybe his next major consignment was already lined up in the sale of Chinese arts and crafts!? With his gall, it seemed he was just as likely to pull off any such deal. Was he really doing all this without the slightest knowledge of the industries he was engaging in! Maybe so because the industry had never heard of him before he pulled that Russian order off!

If ever there were a prize for being the master of negotiation, I would award it to him!

**Key Tactics Summary**

If there is such a list for this example it would simply be the realisation that almost anything can be accomplished given the confidence, the nerve and the gaul.

# Chapter 16
# Negotiating with Banks

A sense of humour can be an astonishingly strong asset, not least with serious bankers. In this chapter I will explain how one of the best deals I ever negotiated got me over the line with a sense of humour and an off the cuff remark.

## What to Request from Banks?

Before approaching a bank, you should have some idea of what terms they might impose, what terms they can grant, and what it is you actually require. You may ask for and obtain a loan or an overdraft, but forget to ask for the icing on top! We will not consider supplementary services here such as safe deposits, insurance advice, and so on but restrict ourselves to the conditions on which we borrow.

Any sum advanced may have the following elements:

1.  Initially the sum required. You will be asked to justify this and may very well have to back this up with a business plan.
2.  What security is asked for and accepted by you. If this includes your domestic property think good and hard before you agree to put yourself and family at such high risk. Flushed with success it doesn't sound so much, but hit hard times and you won't sleep at night.
3.  If you already have a floating charge on your business you won't need to refute a request for security as none could be given, and strangely enough this can work in your favour!
4.  The interest rate, that is to say the cost of money?
5.  What is the interest rate based upon?
6.  At what interval will interest charges be based upon?
7.  Will you be paying simple or compound interest?

8. Does the interest charge incorporate an administration fee?
9. The term. For how long will you keep the money?
10. The currency you are borrowing in?
11. Can you borrow in multi currencies at your own volition?
12. How often is the loan "rolled over"?
13. Whether there is a commitment fee for periods when you do not draw down the money.

These are amongst the main terms that come to mind that I have been in the habit of encountering. From their length you will see that there is much more to the matter than a simple overdraft request that is granted without further ado.

You will also be aware that there is potentially a great deal of negotiating over terms that either side may want. It also follows that unless you are well acquainted with these issues you could be sold a poor deal, or conversely miss the opportunity to obtain a very good deal.

Your accounts, or your business plan, you may be asked to provide will have a major impact on their willingness to lend. Your personality and simple courtesy will be valued highly. You can be certain they will be going over your past, with or without your knowledge, making a full assessment of what risk they feel you may constitute in your own right as well as the business.

It so happens that our two very top directors felt very abused at a refusal they had received only a year or so previously from one of the major clearing banks. My task was to obtain a loan of around ten million pounds in today's values from that very same bank. So something of a cloud hung over proceedings when I first opened negotiations. But Ian, being the kind of man he was, told me of a loan one of the giant companies in the UK had obtained, that he expected me to land for ourselves! That was at only one and a quarter per cent over LIBOR (the London Inter Bank Offered Rate) when most lending could be obtained at anything up to three or four per cent above! Furthermore, this industrial giant had borrowed money for such a long term it compared favourably with share capital, save to say it would be financed by interest rather than dividend payments.

How was I supposed to match that when the same bank had refused his overtures altogether! Surely, I thought, he must be joking!

## The Negotiation

I duly turned up at the local branch to discuss our requirements with the manager. The group accounts I took with me showed a steady increase in profits year on year, largely the result of consolidating results of acquired companies as opposed to organic growth, not that I was going to say as much! From my very early years working as a junior employee in a rival bank I had kept my eyes and ears open, but never formed a very high opinion of the abilities of bank managers to read a balance sheet. It was usually the case that I represented the group in all matters to do with borrowing solo, but following the previous dismal record it was suggested we held a further meeting at high level to consider the application. It would be attended by our chief executive, Sir Ian, the managing director and myself. Now I would have to perform in front of this ever-critical pair, and be expected to bring back results nobody had accomplished ever before!

The discussions took place over lunch when Ian did his usual trick of diverting the conversation to other companies he was involved with, rather than responding to direct questions. The meal was succulent, consisting of the most tender steak followed by delicious strawberries and cream. The general bonhomie was good, and the discussions wide ranging, so hopes were high. We didn't get as far as discussing all the material terms and conditions listed above, but I had made it clear we were looking for long term money at an attractive interest rate. The bank inferred they would advance the loan in principle but when they suggested an interest rate of three and a half per cent over LIBOR my heart sank! Not exactly what Ian expected of me, and I was in no position to fluster and fail in his company. It might also be noticed that the bank focused solely on the rate of interest. Accept that in isolation and I would have given the whip hand to them on all the other terms and conditions cited above! As a negotiating principle never be drawn away from vital terms simply by focusing on the more obvious!

My reaction now was going to determine relations with the bank for a very long term, as well as my standing in the company! I had to find a way of stalling so I could return to the table solo for proper discussions subsequently. Handshakes and smiles were exchanged as we left on friendly terms, but with unfinished business! As we were leaving, I was asked directly what I thought about the offer!

*"Well, I said, the strawberries were fantastic!"*

and we made our way back amongst telling smiles all around, our dignity still intact!

The reader will do well to note how such a disarming but friendly comment is often far better than hours of negotiating your way out of a dead end! But another negotiating lesson here is at all costs to avoid an air of panic. Instead display confidence. A panic-stricken attitude will as a minimum put the costs up. In the worst case it will deny you the request altogether. The strawberry comment avoided both such outcomes in one stroke, and maintained the newly won friendship without killing the transaction off.

The next day a very flustered local bank manager phoned me to say that the bank was really keen to do business with us! I was asked what it was I expected from the bank that he could perhaps assist with. He conceded he had a standard loan contract in front of him, and even invited me to pop down and go through it with him. That was not an offer I was likely to turn down! On arrival he as good as handed me the contract to do with as I wished by way of example of our needs! To coin a solicitors' phrase, I applied the "blue pencil" throughout the draft contract, and left it with the local manager without much hope of success. But if only a part of the revised contract stuck it might still represent a sound negotiation.

To my utter astonishment it was referred "upstairs" and I got everything I wanted! Years later a regional bank director pleaded with me for the right to take it off his books as it "so embarrassed him!" At our very next board meeting I announced the terms I had secured. I had obtained:-

1.   A loan of ten million pounds.
2.   For a term of fifteen years.
3.   Zero security.
4.   Six monthly roll-over periods.
5.   No commission should I not draw down the funds.
6.   Multi-currency.
7.   At one and a quarter per cent over LIBOR.

From the looks of astonishment on the faces of my colleagues I knew I had pulled off something quite spectacular. Of course I didn't expect any accolades from Ian as it was simply not in his character! He sat there with the usual impatient scowl on his face, most probably designed so as to prevent any sign of complacency. That particular tactic I decided to leave to him!

Not so long afterward I approached the major clearing bank that had in my early days been my employers. I was seeking a similar loan on the same terms and conditions. I was introduced to a David Barclay at the very top of the bank. He briefly came out to shake hands and make the odd comment before disappearing back to his office! I was tempted to confess to once being one of his employees but something he said convinced me he was already well aware. For fear of losing the business they agreed to a further loan of ten million pounds on the same terms, being unable to do much else if they in turn wanted any business from us. Now our finances and liquidity was well underpinned, and with no liability whatever to use the funds if we chose not to do so from time to time! Therein lies another important negotiating principle – strike while the iron is hot!

A substantial part of our funding came from the use of acceptance credits, that is to say short term loans usually drawn down at a fixed interest rates for three, six or twelve months. I used these often to back up the longer-term loans on our books and found them very useful. A particular advantage was that, if you had an inkling which way interest rates were likely to go for the next several months you could choose your moment to draw the funds down. So at the first sign or rumour that interest rates had reached the bottom I drew down and borrowed at the cheapest rate for the optimum period, and vice versa. It seemed my judgement was sufficiently keen that it brought a deputation over from the Allied Irish Bank to discover my secret as they complained they never made a profit out of us! But I really couldn't see what was so difficult about moving in the funds market the moment rumours of interest rate changes hit the small print in the press. Wait until it became a stampede and I knew we would by then have missed the boat!

Way back before banking underwent such drastic changes, we were selling an apartment in Hendon and buying an apartment in Barnet. Our purchaser was up to all sorts of tricks and causing mayhem, so much so that the funds never arrived in time to release them to the lady from whom we were buying our property. She was not a well person and had arrived at her new abode sat in a removal van full of furniture only to be denied access. Meantime our buyer was trying to argue the contents of the apartment were hers because we had been using them within the property to sub-let to tenants. She claimed she had bought the property as a letting business and, as such, the contents were hers. This despite us having completed all the usual forms detailing what was staying and what was going as part of the contract!

It seemed the position was insoluble so I relied on two negotiating tactics. Firstly, I told her she had by her actions given us the right to withdraw from the sale, and that since we were having second thoughts about selling that would be our intention if funds were not immediately released. Whilst we waited for her response, we had to find the equivalent of around one hundred and twenty thousand pounds to release funds to the poor lady stuck in the furniture van.

On phoning the bank I was horrified to learn my bank manager was on holiday. I explained that I really needed the funding that very day! Much to my relief they asked me to go into any branch local to my position to identify myself. Meantime an emergency committee was convened and the funds were promised at my disposal by mid-day the next following day! It all ran as smooth as clockwork and the old lady moved in that following afternoon. And we resolved our problems with our own purchaser as anticipated.

Banking isn't quite like that today, but this example will show you the massive advantage of building up a good reputation and rapport with your bankers over the years.

State your case logically and eloquently and anything can be achieved, or at least that used to be the case!


**Key Tactics Summary**
Use humour.
Play one bank off against the other, but in gentlemanly fashion.
Build confidence in yourself and your organisation.
Don't forget the rate of interest is only a fraction of the deal.
Strike while the iron is hot!
Don't present yourself as though you are in a hurry.
Show panic and the cost goes up!
Remember the strawberries!

# Chapter 17
# Consolidating Rights

Benefits and obligations in a group of companies are often quite varied because they have come from different roots from companies acquired over the years. This will inevitably mean that different members throughout such a group have different rights. This in turn can cause administrative problems as well as dissension. So the natural inclination is to rationalize and consolidate them, but on what basis? If each sector refuses to cooperate in relinquishing the best features, then the result will be an amalgam of the very best in each of them, and this will very likely plunge the business into very serious trouble.

So it was potentially when I came to consolidate a dozen or so pension schemes one day spread throughout a group that had grown over the years by a succession of acquisitions. On this occasion the driving force wasn't some envy expressed in one quarter or another, or a union initiative, but the result of Governmental steps to introduce a new State Pension Scheme. We were obliged by law to negotiate with the unions whether or not they should stay in the company schemes or join this new Government State Pension Scheme. I knew even then that I was going to have to keep a dead pan expression on my face in the fervent hope the preferred choice would be to join the State scheme. Anything else and we would be driven into that territory when individual benefits, scheme by scheme, would be compared and argued over.

The State Scheme was going to accrue at a fairly modest rate initially. It would be limited to twenty-five years but there was a Governmental promise it would be reviewed at that time. Both employer and employee would contribute into the scheme. A number of large private schemes had gone into liquidation around the time so the Government scheme, although it was not over ambitious, had the advantage it would not be allowed to go insolvent.

In preparing for my initial negotiations with the unions I made a detailed comparison of all the schemes, their advantages and disadvantages, and prepared for what would follow. If there was one thing I was aware of, it was that union members always placed greater emphasis on what they earned on the day than they ever worried about the future. So I figured they would not be so concerned about the detail of their schemes, even if they understood them in the first place. I also confirmed that an omnibus scheme containing all the best features of all our various schemes would very nearly bankrupt the company. So a great deal was at stake!

My best ploy was to refrain from being seen to push the discussions in any one direction over the other. A gentle nudge in the direction I suspected the unions would naturally opt for was as much as I could countenance. A formal decision was required and I and the unions duly sat down one morning in my office to open proceedings, it not being my usual role to go anywhere near the unions. First task was to explain what the Government were doing and the reasons behind their actions. I knew not to show any pressure or anxiety and the meeting was conducted in a harmonious enough mood. Whilst I could see the flaws in the Government scheme, not least its relatively short duration compared with the average working years, it was not for me to point this out. I merely repeated their mantra that it would be reviewed again in twenty-five years' time. My whole approach was to put them in a position to instruct me on their choices free of any pressure. But I did appraise them of the newspaper headlines they must have seen of industrial companies underfunding their pension schemes and subsequently failing!

I also observed that if any of them should change their vocation whilst in a company scheme, they would lose much of their accrued benefits, whereas they would be free to change employment in the State scheme without any such consequence! Only those giving their allegiance to the company for their entire career would be safe from this eventuality! That observation, on reflection, probably was the nudge in the right direction that clinched the matter.

Much to my relief they came back confirming their decision to drop the company schemes and enter the State Scheme. What was so helpful from a negotiating point of view is that the decision was made simple because it was that of the unions themselves. Nobody was overtly pushing them in one direction or the other. As a negotiating tactic whenever you are fortunate enough to be in this kind of position you should not lose the opportunity to exploit it in similar fashion!

That much accomplished we had to be mindful that a number of executives were nearing retirement on pension rights that were below standard. At the same time if we wanted to attract new management blood then our terms were not likely to be seen in a favourable light. So, as I had hoped, in fact anticipated, now was the time Ian asked me to obtain quotations for a new executive scheme to be limited to senior management.

When we nearly succumbed to the Pilkington bid it was then I had looked around and been offered a position on the main board of Scottish and Newcastle Breweries, a member of the top thirty since taken over by a Dutch brewer. As part of the deal that kept me down south, I was awarded membership of a non-contributory special executives scheme which had been closed to new members for some time. It covered all group service back to my days in the commercial catering subgroup, so any new benefits granted now would swell my fund right back to the day I first joined. So needless to say, I had a strong personal interest in the outcome. Having just avoided a near disaster I felt justified in winning something for myself and my hard-working colleagues.

I knew beforehand there was no way Ian was going to concern himself with technical detail. It was the common belief amongst his subordinates that he regarded himself as something of a demigod. And in any event, he had bigger fish to fry than concern himself with such detail. So I asked our brokers to advise me what officers at the helm of such companies might reasonably expect. Next, I obtained two quotations. The non-executive directors on our main board were of course left out, as was any director already over retirement age, so that only left three of us. I expanded these to include the most senior executives who were not on the main board and obtained a very splendid quotation for such a scheme as befitted this number.

The second scheme would be far superior to anything we had, but was designed for all the remaining managers who did not qualify for the first scheme. A particular feature of both would be a very high rate of accrual. This would permit the long serving executives to enhance their below average benefits to date, whilst at the same time serving as a strong incentive to newly recruited managers. For myself it would hasten the day I could retire which was by stages becoming uppermost in my mind!

Of course I had no doubt Ian would turn down the first scheme in favour of what he perceived to be the more inferior second scheme, a negotiating ploy which served me very well on this occasion. I knew Ian well enough to be able to read him like a book, and it was almost guaranteed he would act as he did. Almost amusingly he conveyed his decision with an air of misplaced satisfaction as though he had driven a very hard bargain, but I hid my utter satisfaction behind a worried frown! He might have had a reputation for being quite the toughest individual to ever negotiate with, but I and my colleagues were well satisfied!

Later on, there would be another twist to this story when I explored the chance of securing inflation indexing to my pension pot by paying for the perk by way of contributing part of my salary. I already had personal salary sacrifice schemes in place and this would enhance my position still further. On approaching the brokers their actuaries determined that a deduction from my salary of seven per cent would be a fair contribution to fully fund the benefit. This was only as much as other executives were paying for their routine benefits, remembering that the deal I struck after the Pilkington bid gave me a virtually free pension anyhow. So how to negotiate this further advantage by bringing my level of contribution up to that of the other members!? I decided to ask John Wiseman as the go-between to approach Ian on my behalf, but was somewhat shocked when I explained my need to John and presented him with the letter of authority which would have to be signed. John, who was serving as managing director as the time, retorted,

*"No point in taking this to Ian, dear boy. Others will only want the same"* (which was barely true in fact as the only other members of equal or superior standing left in the company now were non-executive and extremely rich men in their own right).

*"Where do I sign?"*

asked John, and before I could draw breath, I had a counter signature on my letter of authority from a main board director that now had legal standing! What better example of the advantage of the ploy of using a "go-between" as referred to in chapter four. Despite paying what the brokers considered to be a fair price for the arrangement it was still an uneasy time considering Ian was determined to stay around for a long time!

There was an aspect to this transaction that only I was conscious of! Whilst serving the rest of my career would have fully met the cost of the arrangement, I had no intention of remaining with the company any longer than necessary, but retiring early once the benefit was locked in. The key point being that when the actuaries justified my level of contribution there was no obligation written into the deal that I should stay a moment longer than the first year.

By paying just one year's subscription the indexing would now be applied to all my past accumulated benefits, as I was well aware due to a term in the special pension scheme Ian had agreed as a device to retain my services when I received the offer from Scottish and Newcastle breweries!

True the base salary on which the pension would be calculated would be smaller, but the resultant pension would be more than adequate to support me. This would never have been apparent to Ian even if he had been confronted with the matter since his drive for power made him oblivious to the fact anybody else would place early retirement over and above his thirst for power and longevity!

So my destiny was shaping up very well along the lines I intended, much enhanced by my wit in analysing the opportunities and Ian's inattention to detail! So far as my personal interests were concerned, perhaps my best negotiation to date! I felt a little uneasy but it was a case of each to his own and the proposition had been prepared by top experts in the industry without demurring, all no doubt based on the expectation that we all wanted to continue working till we dropped! It was for others to see the peculiar advantage this transaction granted me in particular circumstances, but nobody was in the slightest bothered by this fact! It wasn't as though the Chairman properly reflected our responsibilities by the salary we were paid in the first place. He had built his reputation on his hardnosed negotiating abilities so this was one way of fighting back both for myself and the other company executives in similar circumstances. But it relied for its success once again upon a discreet line of delicate negotiations.

### Key Tactics Summary

Know the nature of the person you are negotiating with.

Determine in advance what are your aims.

Give attention to the pattern negotiations might follow.

Know the technical stuff.

Offer dual satisfactory alternatives.

Use a psychological approach.

When possible, let your opposite number feel the decision is their so they can hardly have any complaints!

# Chapter 18
# The Way Out

Back at the company, having beaten off the Pilkington bid things were now going to be tough. We had taken over the American Optical subsidiary in Kidwelly, Llanelly, Wales, to avoid leaving a hole in supply that might pull lenses in from the Far East. It was that transaction that had given us monopoly status.

But I never could see how glass lenses immediately in front of your eyes could be a good thing, and had said so ad nauseam. But the alternative plastic lens would always fail until such time we found a coating that would not scratch. For too long the subject had been banned in the boardroom, such that individuals were threatened with dismissal if we raised the subject again! In consequence we hadn't put our backs into the effort. The oft repeated mantra that sand-based glass lenses would always be less expensive to produce than oil-based plastic lenses never impressed me, given the relative low prices at which we sold the basic lenses.

In time the plastic lens argument gathered momentum and the factory at Kidwelly was given over to using the injection method, and traditional CR39 plastic material, but the production never came up to standard. Whilst we wavered the first signs of improved quality plastic lenses infiltrated our market in ever increasing numbers from abroad. Worse still our regular customers were relying on our goodwill to provide them with the more complex glass lenses, whilst taking the opportunity to look elsewhere for lower priced bread and butter products.

An opportunity to catch up was presented through a combination of two things. Firstly, we had a research expert on board who had discovered a cheap translucent material with ophthalmic properties that could be used in producing plastic lenses. Secondly the manager who ran our major manufacturing plant in Northern Ireland tipped me off about a chemical company in Frankfurt that had developed a vastly superior scratch resistant coating. So I took myself off to Frankfurt to meet the executives there and see what could be negotiated.

My first stipulation was that, were we to buy into their invention, we would want the legal property in their coating formula. There was no way, I argued, we could trust ourselves with their product given the millions of lenses we would be producing unless we owned the property in the formula. Of course chemical plants as a rule use all their inventions in multi products so such a request would never as a rule be granted. However, I returned to base flushed with success. At the next board meeting, I rather shocked the technical boffins present by recommending we should abandon our failed attempts at CR39 lenses, and leapfrog the technology. We should use our newfound material for the lens and the coating source I had negotiated. We would use computer-controlled mould filling machines rather than the old-fashioned hand filling methods. The interest was intense. Given that one of our number, Ronnie Hooker, was the current chairman of both the mechanical and the electrical engineering professional bodies he was immediately interested, as were the board as a whole. Everybody looked towards the chairman for his reaction.

Incredibly when he just shook his head in disapproval everybody carried on as though nothing had happened! Exciting as the prospect was it never got off the ground such was the reliance placed on the chairman! I was bitterly disappointed.

The Pilkington affair had left us weakened more than we might ever have imagined. With the penetration of lenses from abroad our production levels were getting out of control, and our stocks rising to dangerous levels. Interest rates were low at the time but a sudden rise would catch us "with our trousers down" and we would pay dearly as I warned the board on more than one occasion. Worse, fashions were changing, and with the advent of much larger spectacles our stocks contained much product that would be harder to move. My criticism of our lack of market research, expressed on the very first day I joined the ophthalmic business, was now being vindicated. At that time, I was informed we needed no market research because, as a monopoly,

*"We were the market! We were the only single authority,"*

it was claimed! But not any longer, nor were the public at large ever consulted!

We had pumped millions after millions into the manufacture of glass lenses. Now those facilities too were becoming under employed! Still the three most senior executives glorified in the name they had bestowed upon themselves, the "triumpherate." But there finally came the meeting when the chair sensed what I was about to say. He tried to pre-empt my inevitable statement by skipping on to "any other business." But nothing now was going to stop me giving the board the facts of life, whether I lost my job in the process or not! I put them on notice that if we didn't reverse the alarming consumption of cash into stock, we would face serious consequences. This was especially so if the economy turned and interest rates suddenly escalated.

The chair had heard enough, not least in front of his non-executive appointees, and the time for action was now! The two other members of the "triumpherate" were charged with the task of sorting the situation out swiftly. To my great relief that brought immediate action and a number of manufacturing plants were inevitably closed down. The stock position improved radically and a positive cash flow of some twelve million pounds was recorded by the end of the year. Strange that some of the toughest negotiations you will ever meet are amongst your own working colleagues and friends!

But there was a cost. Now events were about to take another turn. Our actions necessitated the writing off of stocks, redundancy payments, plant closure costs and so on, so the next published results showed a downturn for the first time ever. The share price fell to a level well short of the historic Pilkington offer, and the chairman felt under pressure to take even stronger action. It seemed to me blame was now being apportioned. My mouth dropped open at the next meeting when he suggested his non-executive directors might feel it the appropriate time to review the performance of the executive! There was only ever going to be one outcome, and the two most senior executives were both pushed out.

Apart from Ian I was now the only one with executive responsibilities still standing on the holdings board. Whilst I engaged as robustly as anybody in our deliberations, my title, apart from being the Company Secretary, was that of Treasurer after an American system Ian favoured which I always saw as a ruse to technically deny me a formal vote if it ever came to that. Neither title in fact gave a clue as to the full responsibilities I carried out, but then that was always a quirk of the way the Chairman operated. According to him my role in particular was to keep a tight rein on the other directors which I could never see quite how that could be relevant exactly. In truth he knew well that there were a number of areas where we were strongly conflicted, and as he was the only executive now with a vote as such, I could only be regarded by him as a threat to his authority. So now our experienced but ageing chairman was determined to "go it alone" and solve all our problems single handed! He had his non-executive directors on hand as usual to back him up, but even they could no longer be relied upon to do so.

Our drop in profits brought a recommendation from the brokers that we should meet our major shareholders at a pre-arranged conference at which we would effectively "sing for our supper!" We were now so thin on the ground that I was asked through a third party if I would be willing to accompany Ian on the day. At the annual general meeting he most often turned to me if he needed prompting over a question, and as a rule I provided him with the response he would rely upon. This meeting, however, was going to be different and I would be standing in front of the shareholders equally open to any questions they fired at me. I had never resented the way Ian and I worked together on such occasions as it protected his status and I felt did me no harm. But I had no intention of just standing there like a dummy feeding Ian with responses without speaking for myself on such an intense public occasion.

I never knew what Ian expected of me because I was never briefed and we didn't speak until the moment we individually arrived in front of the assembled party. Questions came and were answered and the meeting progressed until one comment touched on liquidity. As soon as I started to respond I "felt" a "negotiating tactic" I had never encountered before, or since. I had been kicked sharply in the ankle, and didn't appreciate that particular ploy! I started again only to receive an even harder kick which again I ignored! We got to the end of the meeting finally and left without saying a word to each other.

Even now it was open to us to put our backs to the wall and bring our fortunes around. We were too big to fail and had everything in our favour. But the gap between our share price and that Pilkington had offered weighed heavily on Ian's mind. That chat in the loo was still resulting in reverberations!

I believe at this point, deprived of his two former trusted colleagues, and not getting any younger Ian found himself in an uncomfortable position he would do almost anything to get out of. We never recorded a loss but our profits had suffered a dip for the first time. And it seems any company that suffers a dip is a viable target for acquisitive companies. Before long rumours started to circulate. A good offer over and above the Pilkington offer would at one stroke solve all our problems it seemed. For myself I would always have preferred to ignore any such offers and simply get on with running the company successfully in the conventional way.

The temptation to listen to interested companies was too great, and once the board agreed to do so the word soon got around that "we were for sale!" Now interest in our company grew ever stronger. Came the day when Ian met up with a reputedly successful "wheeler dealer" I was struck with horror! Said gentleman, by his actions, ended up serving a lengthy prison sentence so my feelings were fully justified! Our chairman saw him as a very successful businessman come wheeler dealer, which no doubt he was, but that did nothing to placate my fears!

The way he operated was as follows:-

Firstly, he would meet up with any major company willing to countenance being acquired, usually of course those going through a rough patch. A tacit takeover would be agreed at a mutually satisfactory price. He could afford to fix a reasonable price because it was only ever going to be met with "paper for paper." That is to say with an exchange of shares for shares. The public announcement would impact favourably on both share prices. Disposals of any underused assets would be lined up which, in certain circumstances one might call "asset stripping" but not necessarily so depending on circumstances. Major reserves would be created in the books by way of extraordinary or exceptional items into which all deadwood of the target company would be "buried" or justified post-acquisition. Subsequent results would thereby be that much enhanced. That in turn would elevate the share values still higher, thus supporting more rights issues in the acquiring company placing it in an ever-stronger position to embark on the next such target. It was an all embracing, self-sufficient, self-funding and well-rehearsed scheme that groups in difficulty lined up to take advantage of. And there was indeed such a queue which I was led to understand we had now joined! Perhaps it was the intervention of the Office of Fair Trading that stepped in, or more appropriately the Serious Fraud Office, but the transaction we were apparently warming to never took place.

From that point on it seemed Ian's main ambition in life was to deliver the shares to investors at any price that exceeded that he had denied them in contesting the Pilkington bid. It seemed to me this obsession was now becoming seriously uppermost in his mind. And it didn't help that we were at this stage getting so many suitors who were eagerly lining up to pick the company up at what was a dip in price, albeit a temporary one at that. So when the opportunity presented itself a deal was finally struck with Mo Cuniffe, sole billionaire owner of American Optical in the United States, to offload the business. Different parts of the operation went in different directions. Some became independent. My original commercial catering group was embraced by a fast-growing company interested in less usual product ranges.

One could argue that the "chat in the urinals" impacted in so many ways that the country itself lost a valuable traditional and long-established industry, that once employed over six thousand people. What better evidence that a mere chat in the loo can result in such a major outcome! What better evidence that such apparently inconsequential but often potentially reckless asides play a crucial role in the negotiation process. That the casual comments of one ambitious man can ultimately lead to the unintended but ultimate demise of an entire British industry is proof enough! I personally felt it strongly in my water the moment he proudly confessed to his mischief the morning after the Pilkington celebrations. I knew right there and then that it would give us nothing whatever to celebrate, and history proved me right!

You may ask yourself what if that chat had never taken place; what if a young team had been elevated in time, what if we had leap frogged the plastic lens technology, what if we had sheltered under the Pilkington umbrella in the UK, and a hundred other questions!? Once triggered there is no knowing where such gestures might take you! Once the starting gun is fired the ramifications can be endless, even beyond control. What better example of the huge issues and fortunes that lie at stake, and what better example of the profound importance that this exhilarating subject holds to itself!

For myself I saw what was coming. The company was being sold off under our feet, down river you could say, and nothing could stop what was in train. This epic negotiating trail was triggered by that casual chat, and had now reached a conclusion nobody but the chairman could be seriously happy with. My role in these negotiations was at an end and it was time to move on to fresh challenges. I was looking to move house in any event so it probably came at the best time.

By a quirk of fate, you will read later how I met Mo Cuniffe in New York a couple of years later when he suggested I re-join the board of what had now become the combined UK and US operations. However, right then I had other priorities and had perhaps had enough of the particular industry.

**Key Tactics Summary**
Don't be made a scapegoat.
If there is no other way to progress then stand your ground.
Bring in others in support.
Be careful what you wish for.
Be conscious of "sleight of hand" operations.
Promises made are not always what they seem!
Don't let events get out of hand.
Ankle kicking is not a good look!
Avoid idle chats in the urinals.

# Chapter 19
# On Opening a Railway Station

Watton-at-Stone is a small village you wouldn't notice if you drove along the main road from Hertford to Stevenage, as did some twenty thousand vehicles daily before the bypass was built. The total population was just seventeen hundred, and today is little over two thousand. As such any transport services were virtually non-existent. There was a local infant and junior school but parents had to step in to get their children any place else, more especially for their social lives. To make matters worse the railway line between Stevenage and Hertford, which terminated in Kings Cross, sped through the village without stopping. A station halt had existed but was closed not long before the war, and had since decayed and disintegrated. Only a few dishevelled stones and the odd area of brickwork remained. For the most part the remnants were covered in soil and plant growth.

However, in modern times the line had been electrified. Now engines could stop inexpensively with far greater ease. A germ of an idea came to mind that perhaps conditions might now be right to campaign for a new station. The parish council were aware that Government grants could be applied for such projects, and an application was duly filed and soon forgotten. A word of caution crept in from the outset as it was believed that the County often made such applications under the name of any project which came forward, only to apply the funds once received to other favoured or more plausible projects.

But a considerable time later a letter landed in the Parish Council chambers to the effect the application was now being progressed through the relevant government departments. Residents were invited to form a committee to consider the notion and see if it could be taken forward. I volunteered and joined. Other lay members expressed dissatisfaction over the ponderous way the committee chair was progressing matters, and after general discussion she stepped down and I became the chairman. She had been advocating we hold car boot sales and the like to raise funds, but I denounced such plans on the basis that the sums required were so large, and such an approach would take so long, by the time we had funds the cost would have gone up beyond all recognition far outstripping any monies we could collect through such unambitious means. The moment goes down in history as the start of a string of negotiations that dwarfed most others I had been involved in, not just for the substance of the matter but because of the large number of separate institutions involved.

Our first task was to locate just where our application had got to in Whitehall, so a deputation of us booked a meeting there with our local member of parliament. It was a productive meeting and he promised to try and hasten things along. If we could get the funds to County then we would be in a position to lobby them to make sure they didn't apply it elsewhere, whilst we developed the scheme further.

Back home I arranged meetings with British Rail to discuss the plan in more detail and found them at least sympathetic to the cause. They would after all be getting a new station ostensibly at no cost to themselves if only we could find a way of funding it. Every extra passenger boarding or alighting at Watton-at-Stone would represent added value to them. None of this would have been remotely possible had the line not been electrified in the first place. After a degree of anxious progress chasing, it was finally confirmed that County were in possession of the grant, or at least an undertaking that they would be. We were on our starting blocks!

County back-room staff produced some crude cost estimates, and then came the hammer blow! It seemed they would be well out of our reach, and in no time at all they were indexing the estimates for inflation and the notional cost was getting ever higher by the day! As time went on this practice of applying indexing to estimates continued apace, and no doubt County had already earmarked the grant for something else. It was all too easy for them to surmise the costs were beyond our means, and we were well behind in the race to match them by providing the difference.

But we weren't idle! Right from the beginning we decided to employ the local press to chart our progress. This raised its profile and whetted the appetite of the residents both in the village and its hinterland. However, the road was long and stumbling, and it seemed at every turn, obstructions were thrown in our path. Such obstacles, and our attempts to overcome them, were reported to a sympathetic press. Our station project became a regular feature both in the local papers and even the Times.

We negotiated a "stay of execution" with County whilst we set about exploring other avenues through which we might attract funds. We held meetings at District Council level and added a small sum to the Parish rates through the Parish Council. The District Council pledged a worthwhile sum. Known dignitaries in the area such as the Abel-Smiths were approached and commitments made. We finally set out on a door-to-door collection. There were one or two malcontents but otherwise the effort was well worthwhile. Meantime despite the inflation indexing the gap was closing with the grant, commitments from the Parish Council, the District Council, the village collection, and wealthier individuals now coming in.

A public meeting was scheduled at the County Council offices at which our project was due for discussion. This would determine our fate and it could not in any way be avoided. Special measures would be called for! Firstly, I put the word around that we needed support in the public gallery from as many residents as possible. Next, I contacted the press and arranged for them to be there also. Then I took myself off to British Rail where I could negotiate alone without the distraction of other committee members interrupting proceedings, and going off cue.

The senior executive at Kings Cross and I appraised progress over a cup of coffee. He was informed of the crucial importance of the forthcoming public meeting, and he asked if there was any way he could help. I explained the estimating and indexing methods being employed by County to him, the consequence of which on paper at least damned the project to failure. I pointed out that there would be an expectation that British Rail would have to bear part of the cost themselves, and asked him if they would be willing to put their hands in their pockets in the knowledge that we already had some serious pledges committed. Any such promise from British Rail would remove such a criticism, and pave the way forward!

This much was accepted in good humour. As to how else British Rail could help, I next came up with what any sane person would regard as lunacy! I asked if, in the very last resort, we could be given permission to build the station ourselves! When this was granted, subject only to railway staff supervising the operation, I nearly fell off my chair!

Had there ever been such a request!    Just imagine asking British Rail if residents of a mere village could build its own station, and think how improbable would be an affirmative answer! I even left his office that day with a signed letter in confirmation tucked into my inside pocket from whence I determined it would not meet the light of day until the day of reckoning in front of the County Council!

The public meeting opened on time. All my residents and the press were in place watching every move, and I was asked to present our case. I explained our proposal had been made possible as a result of the monies already sunk in the electrification of the rail. I argued the capital now required would be small in relation to the original investment but produce a useful yield for British Rail, and a much-needed form of communication for the village. Next, I recited the details of all the funds we had raised thus far, and complimented my team on the enormous effort that had gone into the venture. Our prime objective was to point out loud and clear, in front of the assembled villagers and press, that it would be an outrage if "our grant funds" were taken out of our hands and deployed elsewhere.

This led in summary to my asking the County to grant us three pledges:

1. That they would on no account base any decision on purely estimated, indexed costs, without first obtaining at least two or three quotations.
2. That the grant would not be allocated to any project other than the one for which it had been obtained until all else failed.
3. That if, after all that, the costs still appeared too high, then we would be granted the right to build the station ourselves.

Needless to say, the last request was received with incredulity, and the entire room and gallery fell silent.

As the Chairman rose to speak, I had little doubt he would make a showing of some sympathy but then explain how it was all a lost cause! In his mind he was probably already contemplating some sustainable project or other the County required scarce funds for. He would undoubtedly say that British Rail would never agree to anything like that, and of course that was precisely what happened! I had set the trap and reeled him in, and now it was time for the final coup de grace! Of course he had responded exactly as anticipated.

And that was my Neville Chamberlain moment! Out came those famous words!

*"I have here a letter from British Rail you will want to read!"*

I pulled it out of my pocket and, after waving it about a little, I passed it down to the chairman.    There was a stunned silence all around until the implausible truth, the quite impossible, began to sink in.   The shocked silence was followed by a bustle of growing excitement and anticipation as the reality dawned on all those present.

It was checkmate!

Some moments in life you never forget.    This was one of them!

What else could he do!? With the locals and the press all peering at him hanging on his every word, where else could he go now!? I could read that unfathomable look of final acceptance growing on his face. He would clearly now have to change whatever speech he had prepared. I was certain. As it was, he accredited our enthusiasm for the project as much a reason as anything else for pledging the County funds to our station. That last piece of negotiation turned out to be the game winner without question, and keeping it quiet until the last moment gave it the fullest possible impact. Even my committee members were not aware of its existence until it was produced at the public meeting.

There was a moment when I sensed danger, and that was when one of my team members, a parish councillor, went off on a limb pointing out how all our houses would become more valuable once served by a station. The last thing I needed at that moment was an observation that gave the impression we were involved in the project out of self gain. It just shows the difficulties that individual team members can pose if you don't hold it all together, guess what might be said, and take steps to stamp it out at source. That is to say adequate rehearsal. But the moment passed!

Alas I no longer have that letter as the original was kept by the County, and I had not taken a copy for myself. But we all left in a mood of great enthusiasm, the long struggle successfully concluded. We never were called upon to actually build the station. County and British Rail liaised together, and British Rail contributed towards the cost of the materials and labour. After a marathon and a half of negotiations the case was finally won and our role was over. The result was a very handsome new station that still runs today. I am no longer in the region but whenever I pass that way, I take a lingering look at my very own station still standing as a monument to our efforts!

All residents were given a free ride to Hertford and back on the first train to stop, a number of whom had never actually left the village in their lifetimes! The station was formally opened by Sir Peter Parker long before any other communities achieved anything like the same success. I was present for the arrival of the first train but missed the official day since I was abroad on holiday with my family relaxing in the sun! Subsequently the parish council entered the project into the national "Village Ventures" competition. The BBC were present to interview the author on the accomplishment and by way of a little icing on the cake we were acknowledged as the winners!

**Key Tactics Summary**

Go for the greatest impact when it really counts.

Focus your concentration on productive avenues.

Persevere with your negotiations and hang in there.

The press can be your friends.

Pack public meetings with allies to your cause.

Keep the pressure up and be vigilant.

Play your cards right!

Keep your powder dry.

Negotiate with enthusiasm.

Maximise impact.

Keep some cards up your sleeve!

Commit agreements to writing.

Buy a ticket to Watton-at-Stone station from Kings Cross.

# Chapter 20
# Zimbabwe

If you have offices, subsidiary companies or branches which are widespread then human nature is such that untoward things can happen when they are left to their own devices. In the first instance the local management tend to resent being ignored. In time a visit is regarded as an imposition and is in turn resented. After a while, when the team are feeling happier in their isolation, the risk turns to embezzlement.

My brief for visits extended to interests in Europe only, but my desire to get out of our back door was always stymied. Trips to South Africa, for example, were the preserve of a few. But then way back Mugabe seized Rhodesia in a blood bath and announced the new country of Zimbabwe. Hostile actions were ongoing. We had an operation there run by a French manager, Jordan Delourie. He acted under the supervision of Alan Morris who was responsible for South Africa itself. Following the bloodbath, we had little or no idea what had happened to our subsidiary, save to say Alan had caused any cash they had be reinvested in crude iron, safe from the hands of the new regime. Mugabe, on taking power, declared all black persons would be entitled to pension benefits of the same kind enjoyed by whites, but somebody had to explain to the shop floor what that entailed. Knowing I was keen to get out of Europe my chairman made a joke out of seeking a "volunteer," and I was duly elected for the potentially dangerous mission! But I wasn't slow in negotiating with him. I expressed willingness to take on the role providing I was able to buy a round-the-world ticket, and call in on our company in Australia. I knew if I arranged my timetable carefully this would enable me to engage in some stopovers at no extra cost to the company.

I left on Boxing Day, visited a friend in Los Angeles before stopping over for a week in Fiji. Next, I visited another friend in New Zealand before flying over to Australia. An old friend from school days had taken to living up north in crocodile country rather in the fashion of Crocodile Dundee, and I left him to get stuck into company business in Sydney and Melbourne. The Australians were great and I was teased somewhat about their criminal pasts. It didn't take long to realise that if you wanted to negotiate profitably with them you must join in the banter. I boasted that the UK had invented just about all the sports the Australians were so fond of, and they in turn claimed they had taught us how to play them!

On the next leg I nearly got stuck in Bombay for the duration. A handful of us, all on ok confirmed tickets, were directed to a side room, and held there until after our flight resumed without us! I negotiated all night long before I finally found a way of making my way out of the place. Every time any available tickets were announced a crowd of locals numbering hundreds, if not thousands, shot their hands in the air to show passports stuffed with bribes to pay their way onto just about any plane that was about to leave. Negotiation in Bombay was by way of bribe, and I was totally unprepared for this way of life, but now I knew why we had been ushered into a side office! I finally got out of the place after threatening all sorts in the morning. I promised I would get on any plane to Europe to board another back to my destination, all at their expense, and they finally saw the point!

On my return the compensation they offered me in air miles supported a further trip to destinations in the far East. Arriving at Johannesburg the only problem was that my luggage was nowhere to be seen. By the time I filled in all the lost property forms passport control had closed so I walked into the country without further hindrance. My contact was the managing director, Alan Morris. He was an extrovert marketing man through and through. To get any business done I had to cut through all manner of antics!

Alan was married to a Jewish lady and claimed he always kept close to her faith because

*"that's where the money was!"*

How she put up with him I don't know! First thing was to get a feel for what profits he might record that year, but after I had grilled him long enough, he opened a draw, placed a kippot on his head and said it was

*"time for prayers!"*

A smooth negotiator if ever I knew one! After this he proudly showed me his Horse Guards regalia, hung up in a spare office and later we took off to get advice from economists, and visit the bankers.

Next the pension broker arrived at our offices for a scheduled meeting and something just didn't sound quite right! Just how many more times would pension schemes feature in my experiences I pondered.

The funding level of the pension scheme had declined yet at one and the same time it had benefitted from a number of personnel leaving, and a roaring overheated economy. So why had the funding level declined, I mused! It doesn't quite make sense I muttered, excusing myself to attend to the needs of nature.

Alan obviously felt the vibes he thought I was conveying as he cautioned me as to what I was saying. By the time I returned from excusing myself I did so to find the broker confessing to having stolen a million or so from the fund! He had been paying the monthly contribution cheques directly into his own bank account! Now he was beseeching Alan to give him time to negotiate how he would pay the money back! It was a case of that telling chance remark again, but this time with the right effect! The broker must have formed the impression I was not likely to let the matter go once aroused to the apparent quandary, although in truth I would not have had the time to conduct a thorough examination of the books there and then. I learned by this experience that posture is everything! Never forget how chance remarks can have a very powerful influence.

Alan and I continued to Zimbabwe to discuss their pension scheme with the employees as arranged. The plane in front of mine had been blown out of the sky en route to Bulawayo, and the atmosphere was super charged. We were stopped at a crossroads whilst some twenty or more trucks full of fierce looking combatants were being transported, sporting rifles over their shoulders. When you are the only two white faces in the midst of hundreds in a war-torn country, it is hardly a comfortable feeling! The manager, Jordan Delorie, was unable to attend having been fishing in the Zambezi a couple of weeks before, and had contracted sleeping sickness through the tsetse fly.

A few dozen puzzled looking workers were presented to me, and I was invited by Alan to explain the new government policy towards pensions. What I hadn't bargained for was the fact that amongst just a relatively small number they spoke some seven different dialects or languages. Each time I negotiated with the front runners my every word had to be translated from one dialect to the next seven times over! There seemed to be an organised sequence through which this happened ending each time with a rather personable little man at the rear of the room. And any questions he might have came back via the same tortuous route! It was finally that little fellow at the back that complained he didn't want such a scheme. When he retired, he would be granted a cow or a small holding to support him, and assistance from his extended family! So how do you answer that!? I finally explained it was because

*"Mr. Mugabe wants you to!"*

And that was that!

We took time out over the weekend at the Victoria Falls hotel where I watched some erotic native dancing and took part in an entirely different kind of "negotiating!" This time it was at the hands of a crazy pilot in a six-seater tourist plane negotiating his way over the falls and dipping down on one wing into the chasm itself! Despite my vertigo and the recklessness of it all I thoroughly enjoyed the experience. All in all, I was too excited filming and hanging on to even be conscious of the dangers involved!

There was still a little time left of my annual holiday entitlement to join a safari in Hwange safari park before we finally arrived back in Johannesburg in good time for me to catch my flight home. But now I had to negotiate my way out of the country! Not having been able to present my passport on the way in I was now accused of being an illegal immigrant! I seemed to be nothing if not "accident prone!" When they finally accepted my word, I had to go all the way around and present myself at the incoming desks to get my passport stamped. Only then I was finally let out of the country!

On my return to the UK, I circulated my comprehensive report on the trading and economic situation in each country and subsidiary, along with an impressive schedule of savings established whilst on location, but not without failing to mention the embezzlement I had stopped in its tracks saving a very considerable sum of money and employees hard earned pensions. The phone rang numerous times between my head office and the management at the various locations, satisfaction at the long overdue visit being expressed all around. It was all very well received and praise was heaped on my shoulders from all sources, from Ronnie Hooker in particular who reported to the holdings board in person that my tour had been long overdue, and that such a gap in time should never be permitted again! Music to my ears!

But even before all the plaudits had stopped ringing in my ears the following morning my delight was dealt a massive blow by a phone call from the locally appointed Chairman, Harry Swarz.   My joyous homecoming it seemed was going to be somewhat short lived!   The hysterical, almost feminine, ominously high pitch to his screeching voice was enough of itself to be thoroughly disturbing.   What he had to say was worse despite the fact I had never spoken to him before in my life.

Harry Swartz was famous for being the first politician to sponsor anti-apartheid. He attended law school with Nelson Mandela and they had remained very close friends. He led the opposition party for forty years, and had his party won the next election he was widely tipped to become the President of South Africa. That objective was not achieved and in due course he became South Africa's ambassador to the US. He was also a well-seasoned criminal lawyer in his professional life, so a very powerful man I was told you had to be very wary of.

As it was, he had failed to turn up to our meeting when he had been expected. On hearing about the exposure of the crooked broker he went into a temper and it appeared he was giving him his support. Beyond that he took offence that in his absence I had chaired the meeting and minuted myself as such. And when I finally got back to the UK, whilst all the praise was still ringing in my ears, he did his best to get me sacked! That when we hadn't as much as spoken hitherto! For the first time we actually spoke he screamed hysterically at me in a quite unusually high pitched tone that you would have to hear to believe! He told me he was going to speak to Ian immediately and put an end to my career by having me sacked! Something had clearly got to him, and surely a man of his standing could only be acting entirely out of character!?

I was faced the next morning by Ian who informed me I had "seriously upset, Harry," to which I retorted, "He had seriously upset me!" The lateness in the day when Harry phoned was a blessing because, unprepared as I was, it gave me overnight to anticipate my inevitable interrogation by Ian. It was a salutary lesson on the need to anticipate events, and have a response at the ready to enable you to hold your ground. With the benefit of overnight I was well prepared for what would happen next, and as I feared that turned out to be rather challenging. It was as though I was negotiating again for the very job I had already held down satisfactorily for a great many years, but reputations were at stake and the outcome could have gone in any direction!

Ian asked me what I felt should happen about the situation.

I suggested that we could hardly tolerate a local chairman who failed to turn up at meetings which had been arranged in advance at some expense; that we could hardly support anybody that found favour in a broker embezzling from us; that we didn't need a local chairman who refused to carry out the very policies I had been sent down to implement on Ian's instructions, nor did it look good that Harry had arranged a private pension from the company through the same broker he was now supporting without Ian's knowledge. When put to the sword I observed that we could hardly keep him in the position, and Ian had no hesitation in taking my advice and the next day Harry was gone! In his temper tantrum efforts to have me dismissed, even with never having met me, Harry had sacked himself!

And above all else I had now escaped out of my back yard, and would go on to explore the rest of the globe over time.

## Key Tactics Summary

If you accept an obligation bargain for something in return.

Expect a bit of banter in places like Australia.

Make a nuisance of yourself if you are dumped in places like Bombay.

Use bluff if you have nothing else to offer.

Threatening consequences can be a meaningful tactic.

Learn how to judge and react to different temperaments.

When in a hole marshal your defences.

Be prepared to present them cogently and dispassionately.

Never talk down to workers of different backgrounds.

Feigning an insult when none exists is destined to backfire.

Beware marketing fellows who place kippots on their heads as a distraction from meaningful business!

Don't pick a fight you are unlikely to win.

Don't be asleep to risk.

Anticipate trouble and always have a riposte at the ready.

Be fully prepared to hold your ground when under threat.

If you have a potential adversary who has celebrity status prepare well and tread very carefully. Do not leave a stone unturned and always take pains to take the first steps to liaise with potential enemies, however big and powerful they may be.

See trouble coming before it hits you.

Never forget the power of the odd chance remark.

# Chapter 21
# Trading Blocks and Cartels

This chapter highlights the problems and the pitfalls in dealing with public bodies. In this particular case it was the European Union in the early days, but it might have been any trading block. For better or worse I suspect we will never have completely broken our links with the European Union, but I am equally sure that an inkling of how to deal with such bodies will not go wasted.

The competition rules for businesses in the European Union were first set out in The Treaty of Rome 1973. The main principle was that in each member country conditions must be such that all businesses traded with equal opportunities, that is on a "level playing field" as they described it. This meant if you were seen to be artificially manipulating prices in a particular state then the officials could come down very hard on you. That we had companies trading in several member states made us ripe for investigation. So we were not altogether surprised when a formal notification arrived summoning us to cooperate with the officials. The task fell to myself and I was informed we were being accused of charging differential prices from one country to the next. Advice from our solicitors was that the powers wielded by the Union were colossal. They could, for example, close down your entire operation even to the point you went bankrupt if you failed to cooperate with their demands! So in negotiating with them my brief was to be as cooperative as possible.

Before attending at Brussels, I met up with Christopher Bellamy QC, an early specialist in EU law who was in time to be acknowledged as the leading authority in Europe, and was duly knighted for his endeavours. We poured over the Treaty together and I was prepared as well as could be ahead of my initial meeting.

The truth of the matter was we were indeed charging different prices in different countries, but had little choice or control over the matter. Each subsidiary was independent to run its own business as they knew best how. They would charge whatever their particular market would bear, and in any case different specifications meant that products were hard to distinguish in the first place. They did so without any edict from above from us.

The Dutch already felt abused because we had acquired them through a loan financed in their own country, or as they saw it with their own money! Trying to instruct them on their local pricing policy would have been a formidable task in the first place, and we were no experts in their market! So each subsidiary charged arm's length prices according to the competition. That spectacles can also be bought in various states of completion just confused the matter further. And then there were the vagaries of rates of exchange to consider into the bargain.

None of this seemed to cut any ice with the aggressive official, so my first task was to cooperate as planned, and win over his confidence. The first meetings were devoted to my explaining how the entire industry was set up worldwide. I explained who the big players were country by country, their specialties and much besides. He greatly appreciated my efforts to assist, and in due course he came to accept that we had no control over the manner in which our individual subsidiaries set their prices. He also accepted my point that none of them were exactly making anything approaching reasonable profits as one might expect them to be doing had they been exploiting the market.

What happened next was typical of this kind of bureaucracy! The officer was duty bound to issue a formal report. This would either serve as a public commencement of an even more hostile full-blooded investigation which could be very damaging, or on certain conditions I was informed, it would merely report action taken and the case would be filed away! But what action!? We were clearly being let off the hook in return for our cooperation, since the conditions the officer and I came up with between us were meaningless and of no possible encumbrance. The issue was closed and we escaped unscathed.

But it didn't finish at that. I had pointed the finger at Hoya from Japan as being something of a nuisance in their actions to invade our home market. They had opened a factory in Wrexham which is where the officer took himself off to next. Unlike ourselves they put up a fight and refused to cooperate. The next day two large lorries turned up along with a posse of officials, and took away every single piece of paper from their offices. Their entire operation was closed down! We had lived to fight another day but their operation was closed down for the foreseeable future.

**Key Tactics Summary**

Be careful in dealing with public bodies.

Cooperation can be your best tactic.

Argue with logic and find more than one means of proving your point.

Prepare carefully before any meetings.

Start off on the right foot before things get ugly!

# Chapter 22
# Travelling Here and Beyond

With the best will in the world negotiations are sometimes cut cruelly short by unforeseen events. In this venture my partner and I were on the verge of one of the most exciting outcomes I have encountered with major international ramifications, even entering the space race.

During a routine meeting with an executive of Hambros, the merchant bank, I was asked if I would like to join a venture partnering a gentleman linked to the university of Manchester science and technology department who was involved in a rather important project. When I subsequently met him, he introduced himself as Professor John Bather, and we felt an immediate rapport. Our negotiations proceeded amiably and we agreed I should be responsible for all things administrative, organisational and financial and John, as the technical boffin, all things technical. I was still in post but we decided we would start the project outside of normal hours until it grew large enough when we would step down from current responsibilities. First of all, we arranged to go up to the university to view some rather large pieces of equipment in the laboratory.

I stood facing a machine very similar in appearance to that I had stood before many times in my early career in the machine tool industry. At that time, I had been asked by the BSA machine tools group to conclude the acquisition of an electrochemical machinery company in East Grinstead, and bring it up to the BSA headquarters. There I would form a partnership with one Sam Walker who proved to be another exceptional person of like gentle manners. He had been engaged in some amazing negotiations in his career, and it seemed the pattern was repeating itself.

Sam had had considerable experience in the aero industry in his earlier days and was a friend of Barns Wallace, the inventor of the flying bomb used by the dam busters in the war. He worked for Brock aircraft and at one point was trusted with millions of pounds to develop a prototype of a plane, unhindered and unchallenged, within a time scale of a couple of years. During that time nobody interfered, nobody visited the site, and Sam was left quite alone such was his reputation and the confidence they had in him. Who else could negotiate millions to build a plane, and be left to his own devices until he was ready to announce the results!? And he did so weeks ahead of the deadline well within the budget awarded for the project!

Sam was now developing machinery used in electrochemical shaping and de-burring. We could shape anything from false hip joints to propeller blades by electro-chemical machining in an amazingly fast time. The machinery that performed this function was truly exceptional. The unmistakable likeness to the machine I now stood in front of was reflected in the quite large rectangular viewing panel, the rectifier, the sump and its general shape. Within the viewing area of the electrochemical machine would be placed a perfect model of what we wanted to reproduce on the one side, and a blank piece of metal immediately opposite. A direct electrical current passing between the two was sufficient to attract the molecules from the blank towards the model. They never reached their destination because a solution was jettisoned through the gap at sufficient speed to carry them away, and dump them in the slump.

However, the machine now before me turned out to be a mass spectrometer, a very different animal even if outward appearances were not so dissimilar. This machine was used to analyse and determine what any substance was made of from gasses given off from the atoms and molecules of the item under inspection. The objective was first of all to "disturb" the matter in some way so that in doing so it would give off vapour, or gases. This might be by heat, by violent shaking, by bombarding it with "bullets" of some other substance, or a variety of such methods. With the use of electrified analytical tools, the vapours are then routed into another chamber and identified. You learn which elements it is constructed of and the constituent parts.

Our project involved using such techniques to identify bombs or drugs passing through airports for sinister purposes. If all went well, we would be negotiating with all the airports and other key locations all over the world, with governmental departments and with mutual organisations set up under our auspices, covering just about all the spots on the planet. But such a monster of a machine could not possibly be used as it stood. Firstly, it would be very apparent to any would-be bomber or drug smuggler even if it could be so installed, but of course there would never be enough room to house it in that form.

So the name of the game was to miniaturise this substantial piece of machinery down to brief case size. That was the project that John Bather was engaged on and upon which he was already very far advanced. A prototype had been created which we carried around with us from place to place engaging in preliminary discussions with interested parties. At this point so far as we knew we were the only parties in the world engaged in this activity. It was only later that a team connected with Cambridge university, if I recall correctly, first embarked along similar lines. And much later before anybody in the US got word of what was happening here.

It is a matter of record that when John and I drove around these locations he invariably did so without his seat belt placed around him. As "negotiations" go it barely justifies the description, but I pleaded with him many times to take sensible precautions. His answer was always the same.

He was afraid that in an accident he would end up caught up in the seat belt, most probably with it around his neck!

And then, at the height of his career, and on the eve of all his amazing work, disaster struck. He crashed badly and the damage to his brain was such that he ended up more or less in a vegetative state. His body recovered enough that he could swim up and down the pool under supervision, but he hardly knew his name and it was the end of the project for us both.

Subsequently others carried on and, although I am ignorant as to the extent of their use at airports and the like today, I do know that such miniaturised mass spectrometers are built into the exploration machines that advanced countries are sending out to the planets right now. The machines in question have a drilling device that drills into the topsoil or rock and brings the samples up into the mass spectrometer for analysis and relaying back to Earth, more or less instantaneously. The machines are of course miniaturised but carry out exactly the same function that John Bather was working on. His machine might well have been the first to enter outer space!

I used to enjoy a pint or two with a rocket engine scientist who frequented the same local as I in my village. He was responsible for the design of rocket motors used to get to other worlds, as well as the motors used in those machines that scour the surface of far distant planets. They tell us if there is water to be found, what kind of gasses abound, and much more that one day may support humans on other worlds. One wonders what kind of conversation we two might have had if the results of our combined operations were conjoined in a single device heading out to space!

It just illustrates how far successful negotiations can take you, even though, as in this case they were brought to an untimely and abrupt end. I am fully confident that without demonstrating negotiation and presentation skills over the years I would never have been singled out for the honour of accompanying John Bather in the first place. From that banker's office in Bishopsgate what followed had the potential to impact on the safety of international travel throughout the world. Where we had to adjourn from the activity others followed. It is an example of what rewards and pleasures can stem from negotiating credentials and an awareness of what is going on in the world! A great pity we were not left able to negotiate with all the airports around the world on the means of keeping them safe.

### Key Tactics Summary
If Sam Walker could single-handedly take responsibility for pioneering an airplane then anything is possible!
Use your negotiation skills, never let the task phase you.
When you negotiate with your character and the trust it engenders outstanding opportunities can follow.
What a shame my attempts to talk John Bather into a seat belt fell on deaf ears!

# Chapter 23
# Dangerous Liaisons

So far we have followed the tactics used throughout negotiating when tangible benefits to each party were at stake. But there are situations when your very life may depend upon using the right tactics at the right time. Such as the time when I was with friends at a jazz club in the Stork pub in Walsall. The band was known as Ken Ingram's Eagle Jazz band and the place was well attended, the atmosphere second to none. After downing a couple of pints, I needed to go to the gents.

I arrived to find them spacious but deserted. As I stood at the urinals some instinct, the flicker of a moving shadow, I will never be sure put me on edge. Something just didn't seem right. I turned to see a horrible gaunt twisted looking individual standing immediately behind me, arm raised with a vicious knife about to be plunged into my back! As long as I live, I will never forget the contorted evil sadistic insane look in his face, as though he were possessed by the devil himself. Whatever was going to happen now was going to happen in a split second, so my life depended on my sharp thinking and the right response. Should I parry the knife and get into a vicious fight, in which case I would be totally unarmed. Should I turn on my heel before the knife plunged and make a run for it, in which case I probably wouldn't get past the door!

My assailant had obviously hidden until that moment in a closet. Whilst I was completely unprepared, he on the other hand had the advantage of not only holding a weapon, but knowing what he intended to do with it! I chose neither option in the event, and instead addressed him, deciding a psychological approach was my best bet. As I turned he initially opted to palm the knife as best he could out of sight. I knew it was important I shouldn't draw attention to it or he would most likely panic and use it anyhow. I knew a subtle negotiation was called for so I decided to address the matter verbally. Looking him sympathetically directly in the face I asked him,

*"Are you alright, mate?"*

And that was enough!

Confused that given the situation somebody should express concern for him was all too much! He turned on his heel and ran for the door. Once through he charged through the gathered crowd, his palmed knife protruding out as he thrashed his way along leaving a trail of blood behind him. Handbags were slashed and dresses ripped apart but fortunately the wounds were for the most part superficial. I followed immediately behind until I reached my friends, by now aghast at what they had seen. I was cross examined as to what exactly I had said to make him run amok in such a fashion.

*Oh,*

I said, as though a massive understatement

*"Are you ok mate!"*


Then something occurred to put that story in the shade. I was attending the centenary of my commercial catering company employers, WM Still and Sons Ltd. I give the name because it is an integral part of the story. The function was held at the famous "Inn on the Park" hotel in Park Lane, London. The company now assembling were in the main elderly retired members of the original Still family. They had all long since been disposed of by the new business owners on takeover, save for the managing director.

Carelessly I got out of the lift one floor higher than I should have, and found myself facing a single door bearing no signage. I wrongly assumed it would be the way through to the banqueting hall. Instead, I found myself in the middle of a lounge which I was horrified to realise was part of a private apartment. And before I could blink a very elderly man came from nowhere stooping to gather a trail of toilet paper at every step. He had obviously placed them there in the first place and was now retrieving them. His finger and toenails seemed inches long, and he wore a long white nightdress down to his ankles which looked as though it had come right out of Dickens. He wore a white nightcap folded over his ear to match. He was stooped and wizened, altogether the strangest sight I have seen.

His mood seemed very preoccupied but when he drew level with me, he showed no surprise, and little fear. I could just about discern an acknowledgement of my presence when he drew attention to something hanging on a chain around his neck. He muttered in a barely audible voice

*"Here, do you want a million?"*

Before I could gather my senses, he carried on his way and left me rooted to the spot. However, the mood soon changed when I felt the solid thrust of a gun barrel pressed into my back. Hoodlums had taken over control of the old man who was enormously rich, and it was one of them that now held the gun firmly into my ribs. I was told to put my hands up whilst they frisked me, and to keep them up whilst I gave an account of myself.

It was slowly beginning to dawn on me that I had encountered the then richest man in the world, Howard Hughes.

It was well known that he or his controllers rented the top floor of the hotel. But nobody ever saw him. In order to keep his whereabouts secret at all times the hoodlums would smuggle him in and out of the country in a coffin with air holes to keep him alive. Clearly it was he, and the "million" he offered me the blue diamond, the most valuable in the world. Howard Hughes had fallen into the grip of the American mafia, for want of a better description, and they kept absolute control over his fortune and his person. To this end he was drugged out of his mind most of the time. What I had seen was a closely guarded secret from the world. Others that stumbled upon the truth had, it was rumoured, ended up in a concrete foot bath at the bottom of the river Thames, forced to sit with their feet in a bowl of cement until it set, and then being dumped into the river!

How to negotiate my way out of this situation!? There was a great deal of shouting at absent guards who should have been at the door. There were recriminations that they had rented only the top floor when they should have bought the whole (expletive) building. When I was asked what I was doing there I fortunately had a verifiable answer! I had been frisked and remained stood there, gun in my back and hands still aloft when I spoke. My tactic would be to treat it as an everyday occurrence since to show outrage or appear to rebel would I feel have sealed my fate.

With an air of confidence, not showing a flicker of annoyance or concern, I spoke those immortal words that most likely saved my life. Perhaps representing the most important negotiation ever!

*"I'm here for the WM Still and Sons Limited centenary celebration."*

Try saying that with your arms in the air and a gun in your back! For some reason whenever I am asked to repeat the story for friends or acquaintances my other half thinks that line is extremely funny.

*"We might never have met,"*

she cheerfully tells me! And I remind her that it wasn't she that was facing a concrete foot bath, and a dip in the Thames!

A thug was sent down to the correct floor to verify I was expected. I got a good dressing down and apologised profusely before joining the party, but not without choosing to ignore the muffled shouts of the prisoner obviously being administered drugs again to keep him quiet! In time I wondered if he had wanted me to take the diamond as an indication to the outside world as to his plight. On arrival at the function, I sat next to the development director, Michael Phillips (Michael Phillipovic in his native Polish).

*"A strange thing happened to me on the way here,"*

I started to say, but the managing director was already on his feet welcoming Aunt Floss on her zimmer frame, and all the other "Stills" so the moment passed. I never told the story to a living sole for many decades and just got about my business, too busy to look back!

As part of my role, I would often have to travel to our major manufacturing plant in Northern Ireland, and it was during the period of the "hostilities" as they had become known. The driver picking me up drove at a reckless speed. I used to think of him as a bad driver until one day he conceded he was doing so to avoid a bullet, or worse an ambush! One night I was moved from my regular hotel because it was hinted we would be victims that night. Both sides paid what was thought of as "alimony" or shall we say "protection" monies to preserve venues they had an interest in. I was always more than pleased to get back to base in one piece. Then one morning in our offices in London my managing director approached me looking rather rueful.

*"What would I do if I found I was on an IRA hit list?"*

I was asked. The terrorist organisation had been kidnapping industrial leaders as a means of extracting a ransom, and one of their number inadvertently dropped the list from his pocket to be picked up by the police. When I declared I would "run a mile", I was clearly adjudged to have failed the "loyalty test!" What kind of a negotiation was that!? Fortunately, they got little change out of that policy and the kidnappings ceased!

My next uncomfortable situation was a result of something we had discovered in our systems surveys at Fort Dunlop again. It was known that tyres were being regularly stolen from the Fort. The task was to find out how this was happening and to plug any gaps in the system. A man fishing in the polluted river running at the rear of the stores drew attention to himself when it was discovered he was "fishing" for brand new tyres in a polluted stream that hadn't seen a fish for a lifetime. His accomplice from within was throwing them into the river from which they would have floated down to the location of the "fisherman," but that was small beer.

More significantly the weighbridge records showed discrepancies between the theoretical weight of consignments and the actual tonnage, and it was found the difference was accounted for again by stolen tyres. And on the floor of one of the trucks, security picked up a fully typed "order" for stolen goods on professional-looking letterhead from the criminal underworld! The lorry was seized and the culprits dealt with through the courts. By one of those astonishing coincidences one day, I was sitting having a beer in a local pub I rarely frequented when I overheard somebody openly negotiating prices for Dunlop tyres! It was hinted without much attempt to disguise the facts, that such tyres "could easily be obtained!" Observing my growing interest in the conversation attention reverted to myself, and I made a hasty exit to report the incident later!

Once when I was hitchhiking home during national service I unwittingly stepped into a very handsome car, possibly a chauffeur driven Bentley, or the like, containing no less than all three of the notorious Kray brothers! At points the brother adjudged to be schizophrenic, Ronald, was showing signs of frustration and far too much of an unbalanced interest in myself, enough in itself to put me on high alert.    I decided the best ploy would be to chat as though they were any ordinary members of the public, and the conversation soon got around to conscription. I would not for a moment disclose that I was aware who they were.

So my negotiating objective in the circumstances in which I found myself was to simply keep the atmosphere calm by virtue of my conversation and the demeanour I adopted.

We were all at one over our feelings towards conscription, the twins having been so unruly in their time in khaki they were dishonourably discharged! They were on their way to Birmingham to plan the opening of night clubs, so I struck a chord by enthusing about their prospects before I happily thanked them for my lift and stepped out, grateful to be in one piece! The tactic of building a rapport had served me well, as it most probably would with most folk in a similar situation. It takes a fairly placid but shrewd personality to go around the world building good relations but I have never found the effort wasted. Had I put a step wrong that journey could quite easily have been my last!

It was during another trip to Nairobi that I was staying in the capital, and about to take the plane home the same day. Walking around the city was somewhat daunting because I appeared to be the only white face I could see in all directions. As I strolled along two men, who turned out to be Tanganyikans, approached me. They used racial prejudice as their prime negotiating tactic. That is to say if I wouldn't take a coffee with them they argued, then I must be racist! I foolishly relented and we found our way to a coffee bar nearby. Once inside I was told they had gone AWOL from their army which was at war. They had no money, no passport, and needed help and an address in the UK.

I refused to be drawn and suggested we left. They led the way out via what must have been the back stairway since it ended up at a tarmac area at the rear of the building, and now I was at their mercy! They first walked alongside me and then fell back behind me, and I quickened my step. They did likewise until it got to the point we were almost running. At this point I glanced behind me and could see sunlight glinting off the blade of a sinister looking weapon! Seeing me turn one cautioned the other to withdraw. We walked ever faster until I finally broke into a run. There was no hiding the situation now to anybody. They did likewise and I feared the worst. Much as I could sprint, they caught up with me, but to my utter relief ran quickly past me, and through the gateway to disperse amongst the crowded streets! I was to learn subsequently that had they been seen at close proximity plunging a knife into me it was the custom for the crowd themselves to mete out their own street justice on the spot! I had just made it close enough to the public street to save the day.

It had been my desire not to appear racist that got me into that trouble, that is to say to conform to public opinion. But there are times when conforming with public opinion can not only hurt your pocket, but even put your life at risk as I had discovered! Better to assert you are not what they regard you as and stick to that line as non-negotiable.

My fiery boardroom colleague, of whom mention has been made in chapter fourteen, the one who had eliminated more of the enemy in World War two than I had had hot dinners, had set his sights on acquiring a defunct company in a transaction I was totally opposed to. He was one and the same who thought good marketing was to storm around to a complaining customer and knock him clean out.

What really troubled me was that the vendor had requested we should permit him to retain the accumulative tax losses for his own deployment, whilst we would pick up the almost impossible task of turning the company around. Having discussed this with the other key executives outside the boardroom I was ready to make my stand when I saw him, whisky in hand, storming towards me. I was stood in the midst of shareholders and dignitaries after a very formal AGM lunch chatting to a leading general manager of National Westminster bank when he finally reached me. Not wasting a moment my fierce little friend tore into me, and as I defended my actions his retort still rings in my ears today!

He drew himself angrily up to his full height of five feet four inches, if my memory serves me right, and spat out,

*"Have you ever killed a man?"*

The look on his face betraying the fact he would have loved to finish me off there and then! Of course we all knew full well he had done as much in numerous heroic situations throughout the war, and for which he received many decorations. Rather an embarrassing situation, given I was talking to one of the few men whom we might subsequently rely upon to finance our business.

My fiery companion then eased the temperature somewhat by clenching his fists and protesting

*"If only I could reach up to you!"*

But then he took another mouthful of whisky and you could read the change in his mood, as you always could after a given level of spirits had been consumed. His eyes functioned as a guide to his mood since at a given level of spirits they would conspicuously harden and it was time to risk all or get out fast!

Suggesting it was the whisky that was talking proved to be quite the worst negotiating tactic in the circumstances! On doing so John spluttered out

*"How dare you suggest I'm drunk!"*

It was quite the most difficult situation to negotiate oneself out of.

My ploy was to give him enough licence to talk long enough before he exhausted what he had to say, and wandered off to fill his glass again!

Strangely enough we never did business with that particular bank and it was as well I had plenty of other sources! What their senior general manager had thought of one of our main board directors can only be left to speculation.

My aggressor never carried out his threat or I evidently wouldn't be here writing about the incident again, and it was forgotten as soon as the whisky stopped talking!

Subsequently we worked closely together and formed a very friendly relationship. Later still John gave an option on his shares to yet another person who had been led to believe a takeover might be possible, but then told the opposite! His actions were deemed to be treason of the highest degree and at his final board meeting we were each in turn given the opportunity to castigate him. As it was, ever since he first committed his company to join the group, he had only ever received shares for shares, and I was witness to several occasions when he was told it was not the appropriate moment to cash in any shares without damaging the company. Having tried to negotiate this numerous times he was now being drummed out of the company for having jumped the gun! Each member duly expressed bitter resentment at the invitation of the chairman, his brother included. I was the only one who sat grimly silent my lips sealed tight!

One wouldn't normally take a holiday in North Korea but my travel lust took me right down to the infamous 38$^{th}$ parallel between the north and the south a decade or so ago. The buffer zone here is regarded as the most dangerous place in the world, and the concentration of nuclear bombs and conventional weaponry on land and sea is immense. For a short distance only fencing and little more separates the American troops from those of North Korea. In the centre there is a hut which straddles both countries, and which is intended as a meeting place should it ever be agreed both sides should face each other around the table.

I was shown around by the Camp Commandant, the most senior ranking military officer responsible for the troops on the border, which in turn makes him one of the very top officers in the entire North Korean army. At first, he looked me up and down suspiciously, and never relaxed the fierce look he carried with such pride. It took a little while to break the ice, but I acted quite naturally and the atmosphere eased. And "ice" was the operative word since it was absolutely freezing. Earlier my guide had driven me down the major link road from Pyongyang. As we proceeded along, we saw villagers scraping the ice off the road with blunt instruments such as ordinary cutlery knives and spoons at six in the morning. This was the enduring responsibility of each village the road passed by, and there would have been the most severe repercussions had any stretch of road not been clear.

It was in that intense atmosphere that the opportunity to gain the officer's support presented itself when he took me outside to view the American soldiers patrolling the other side of the divide. Except to say there were none there, no doubt because of the severely low temperatures. I quipped,

*"The Americans won't come out in the cold"*

and the manner in which the remark was received was remarkable. I was suddenly accepted as a colleague and an ally. I sat at the desk within the hut and made out as though to sign a peace treaty between North Korea and America, whilst the officer himself obliged by taking the photograph! I could hardly believe we were "play negotiating" something the world so desperately wanted.

When I left, he summoned his three most senior subordinates to his side. On his command they all gave me a highly polished salute! Feeling that kind of empathy that anybody who has served in khaki feels, albeit only as a conscript, I smartly retuned the salute, and I left to find my guide for the drive back to Pyongyang.

Whilst the officer and I were pretending there were plenty of high-ranking officials within the country who would have given anything for a simple joke which might have saved their lives! As for my dig against the Americans, made in jest given where I was, it certainly set the right aura from which serious negotiates might have continued. But I was there on holiday, and I doubt the USA would have approved of my actions! Nevertheless, in the circumstances the ploy seemed tailor made for the purpose, and I doubt I could have come up with much better!

**Key Tactics Summary**

In danger the approach you take is crucial.

Think on your feet.

Psychology can be a good friend.

Conceal your anxieties or you may accelerate reprisals.

Employ that spirit of bon homie at all times.

Don't be goaded into situations against your instincts.

Don't be a slave to public opinion.

Anticipate, but be prepared for the unexpected.

Acquire skills to handle fiery or intoxicated opponents. Don't let them scupper your negotiations!

Think in the "language" of your opposite number.

If you get "hit listed" don't fail the loyalty test!

Learn how to run fast when all else fails!

# Chapter 24
# Joining a Stock Market

It is perhaps not surprising how far owners of companies will go in pursuit of their interests. This example involves a very specialist business that manufactured machinery for operating mine shafts and large engineering projects, and which provided a full range of bearings used in the moving parts themselves. There was something of an affinity for me with anything connected with the machine tool industry, but it was my recognition of a local landmark I believe that got me the job. It unexpectedly became an important part of the job negotiations, rather along the lines of the return of the prodigal son! Whilst the interview was taking place, I found myself glancing out of the window at a local Midlands landmark. On asking if we were looking out on the Clent Hills, a warmth came over the meeting that I doubt most other applicants enjoyed! Here I was, not necessarily in my favourite place on the planet, being welcomed home!

The two sole owners had ambitions to expand and had been advised to join the Unlisted Securities Market, since defunct. Underwriters were unwilling to support the listing until a finance director with City experience was on board, so I was duly elected at great cost to the company. I had my parents living with me in an annex and it was no longer a practical plan to move into a joint property. So when I made my acceptance of the job conditional on the company meeting much higher removal costs, even down to paying the interest on the bridging finance on my mortgage, they readily agreed. After all they would become paper millionaires overnight and they couldn't wait to get started.

For my part I was lured by the very strong hint that I would succeed the managing director when the chairman retired and he took his place in the not-too-distant future. In the course of time this would turn out to be a hollow promise, but the word would get around just the same and caused much resentment amongst those already established in the company. The company had a very jaundiced view of those emanating from my profession, and I very much doubt if I or anybody else would ever have been appointed were it not for the listing on the stock exchange. So whilst both sides fulfilled their immediate short term needs it was an uneasy alliance that turned markedly once the listing on the exchange was complete. The company's purpose having been achieved I felt I was experiencing a marked change in the atmosphere. It taught me you must always be careful when negotiating career moves of the sting in the tale and of unspoken caveats that manifest themselves in the course of time!

Whilst I had been serving my notice the company had acquired a competitor in the same heavy engineering industry specialising in crane equipment. The handsome price paid for the acquisition had drained a significant share of the liquid sources on flotation, was costing interest, and also rental for the areas its defunct machinery was occupying. What was worse was the fact that the two companies were the only ones of any significance in this specialist industry. Had the company just sat around whilst the weakened competitor went into liquidation, as it was in the process of doing, then the business could have been picked up without as much as lifting a finger or a penny being spent!

This poor investment choice was the brainchild of the director running that branch of the business. It seemed to me he was treating the ambition of restoring the plant that came along with the purchase as something of a hobby, to be visited from time to time when he became bored! Those particular machines were never needed nor utilised, instead just sitting there occupying space for which we were paying those high rents.

I was somewhat annoyed that they had proceeded with the transaction without once trying to canvass my opinion whilst I was serving my notice with my old employer, and I made no attempt to conceal this. As it was the director concerned was already jaundiced against anybody from my profession, even to the point of banning the newly appointed young accountant from attending his meetings on the grounds others on the shop floor had longer service! And there were plenty of others who could never come to terms with the fact that, as an outsider, I myself had leap frogged them directly onto the board of directors. It was certainly one of those environments in which you had to watch your step! Then somehow the other directors had got wind of the fact I had been tipped as the successor to the managing director, and I was challenged directly whether this was true!

It was all a hotbed of dissent with all the feverish negotiating taking place in house and out of hearing. Managers negotiated their way up the tree at the expense of others. Any minor indiscretion on anybody's part was stored, exaggerated, and used to further the interests of the aggrieved. Situations were contrived to further the cause of ambitious individuals. Progress was negotiated through the proverbial knife in the back! The general scenario was one of mean-minded people edging their way upwards on the shoulders of others. They were all too consumed with their own interests to see that anybody from outside would ever have the special experience required in the situation. It was one of those businesses wherein the whole atmosphere was poisoned, and not one in which I wished to remain any longer than it would take to see them through becoming a public company.

This was one example of a number I had experienced over the years when heavy handed owners think they have the right to tell you what the profit is going to be before you have as much as put pen to paper. Of course, with a listing on any stock exchange it is necessary to give a profit forecast, and it is indeed quite true that to fail this forecast presents you with potentially serious difficulties. But to think such individuals can chose the profits calculated at their own whim, and instruct me as to what it should be is beyond the pail! The duties the accounting profession are responsible for discharging are strictly non-negotiable! That they attempted to do so was just about the final straw. I felt I had been used for their prime purpose of obtaining a listing, and now they were showing my profession itself disrespect.

They had entered the stock market in a frenzy of excitement at becoming paper millionaires, but found the environment anathema to them. Their purpose had been served, but begrudgingly so, and my ongoing costs were beginning to rankle! Both sides had achieved their aims so we had reached a win-win position at the outset, but now the honeymoon period was over! My personal need to sell my old house, move home, and house my parents separately had been served well whilst they had got their listing. I had moved into a new property suitable for the long term, but some considerable distance away in the short term whilst I remained at the company. That much negotiated and cemented I decided other needs were calling. So I set myself up as a consultant and moved on at no further loss to myself or my dignity.

The chairman and I had attended a stockbrokers meeting in front of potential investors in the City, but he point blank refused to answer any questions. When I was asked six times what my feelings were about the company's prospects, each time the chairman killed off my response before it left my lips. This type of pre-planned meeting is in the nature of a gentle nudge or understanding that you have something to offer the potential investors lined up to hear your story. But any such understanding was killed on the ground. Instead, bored participants turned their curiosity to why it was I had left my previous post. Gleaning any meaningful information from my new employers seemed an impossible task.

Eventually the owners bought back their shares and were released from the merry go round of brokers meetings they concluded had "no right to pry into their business!" In time under new management, they did go on to make substantial profits but remained forever a private company.

### Key Tactics Summary

Don't get a listing unless you are prepared to play by the rules. These are not negotiable!

Being promised a future promotion can be a poisoned chalice! Deny it or keep it under wraps at all costs!

Knowledge of the local area can influence your interviews.

Look into the minds of management before you plunge in!

Don't be naive as to the intentions of those around you.

Bide your time to earn your rewards.

Be prepared for anything.

Don't drive too hard a bargain on moving. Once the original purpose is fulfilled the costs are resented.

Keep your cards close to your chest.

Anticipate resentments and handle them with care.

Toughen up or get out! Don't flog a dead horse!

# Chapter 25
# The Management Buy-Out

This section carries a public health warning! It involves support from a merchant bank in a management buyout at the retail end of the spectacles market. It involves a labyrinth of negotiations that dwarfs all the others by a fair margin!!

As a private company it was owned by an optician and his wife whom I had hosted at a hospitality meeting at the York races in an earlier capacity at the mass manufacturing end of the product. The couple were buying lenses from Hoya, the Japanese company, and it was causing consternation with my previous employers. The faster they grew the more business we were missing out on, and they had already expanded into some two hundred branches. The kind of hospitality event I attended was covertly an out and out negotiating ploy to attract new customers. Those representing the hosts sell their personalities in the hope there will be a payback at some point in the future. And now I found myself applying to them instead for employment to meet my short-term needs!

Their requirement was for somebody with mature business experience, but in particular for somebody well versed in raising funds. I lived locally and knew the industry, as well as having met the owners, so it was a good match.

The industry had changed much over the previous decade or so. In the old days somebody requiring spectacles would first go into high street opticians for an eye test. The atmosphere was usually formal and there was no chance you would be let out the door with your prescription in your hand. This was to stop you from shopping around to buy your spectacles elsewhere. After the test they would sit you down and produce just one or two models they felt appropriate. You would be invited to try them on, and complimented on how well they suited you. Only once you were hooked on a particular model would you finally be told the price!

Then in a new development, notable personalities at that time such as Barbara Castle and Esther Rantzen raised complaints about the price of spectacles. They were not, as it happened, comparing like for like and practices abroad bore no relationship to the home market. Nevertheless, the pressure brought enduring changes. If opticians wanted to survive, they would now have to set up a comprehensive range of frames the customer could view. They would be labelled with their prices so that the customer could make an informed choice to suit his or her pocket. And now the customer could take his prescription away and make his or her purchase wherever they thought fit. So it followed that retail opticians with ample space would do well in setting up their displays. The new competition drove down prices and the policy was working well until the Government got greedy. Even before the dust had settled the Government carved out their share of the bonanza by adding value added tax, and by causing the customer to pay for his own sight test. Major optical outlets now offered other features such as speed of delivery, special optional tests and other such features.

The owner. Whom we will call Oliver had seen a parallel system working in the United States, but through major store groups wherein the customer could browse unimpeded, and combine this with day-to-day shopping. He came back with the idea and put it to Woolworths who decided to launch it as soon as possible. Oliver was told he would be expected to establish up to two hundred outlets within the major Woolworth high street stores. He would first of all be expected to create a factory operation with equipment and staff capable of serving the orders received through the two hundred sales outlets. Oliver set about the task with a vengeance despite his peers regarding him as undesirably avant-garde. This was a dramatic departure from the traditional high street opticians of the past, and looked upon with disdain by the rest of the industry.

The factory was wholly financed by his own funds or an overdraft. That it was funded to such a degree by an overdraft that could technically be recalled at any moment was a fundamental mistake, and I think most would have regarded the bank manager's acquiescence to such an arrangement rather irresponsible. Woolworths permitted occupancy fees to roll up without undue pressure, largely because they had half an eye to converting the debt to share capital if the project was to become a major success.

The Tory member of parliament, Ken Clarke, came along to officiate at the opening ceremony for the new plant.. The company growth rate was phenomenal, but in view of the commitment to Woolworths it was an unavoidable fact that Oliver had all his eggs in one basket! As the total debt grew higher and higher the cash through the till was ploughed back into new branches, baulked up by deferring payment of creditors. Obvious pressures were building in all directions. Whilst Oliver's reputation was growing fast the bank manager was not quite so sanguine. He met me as I arrived at the door to inform me he was about to pull the rug on the company unless I came up with a solution! A rather pointed negotiation one could say!

Meantime Oliver had given the deeds of his house over to the clearing bank as security and didn't know which way to turn. My brief from him was to do whatever it took to get him out of the mess. That could be in the form of bank finance of one kind or another, joint venture capital, by offloading some of the shares, just about anything included selling the company outright! The inexhaustible round of negotiations had just begun! The incumbent managing director we shall refer to as Brendon. He seemed to naturally team up with me and we worked together to try and find a solution. And all the time the rest of the industry looked on with envy and admiration at the rapid growth Oliver was attaining!

I worked tirelessly to find the right solution and it wasn't proving easy. Oliver, as desperate as he was, voiced objections to certain solutions. And the fact he was already so substantially in debt didn't help the cause. Then a rare opportunity came along to open discussions with the billionaire Mo Cuniffe in the United States. He was the very same who had acquired my old plc company. Added to American Optical in the US the two together now formed an even bigger operation. It was Brendon who somehow made contact with him and I spoke to Mo on the phone the next day. In result I was offered a meeting in Rio de Janeiro of all places since he said he would be down there for a few days, and understood our urgent need.

When he learned I would be flying back on the same plane as himself he suggested we meet on the flight. He "would give me an answer before we got off!" he promised! Never in all my days had I flown so far as Rio to negotiate with a stranger on an airplane on the return journey! That was surely the most astonishing insight into highly successful billionaires who can negotiate "on the hoof!" I was of course yet to see if he lived up to his word!

I was more than a little hesitant to spend the company's money on such a way out means of doing things, and said as much, whereupon Mo offered me two hours in New York the following day providing I could find a way of getting there on time. Something had to be concluded at speed because Woolworths had finally entered the scene and were about to make an unsolicited offer to take over the company, or a major part of it, in lieu of the debt owed for license fees.

Allowing for the time difference I could just about do it if I flew Concorde, and I luckily got the last available seat. I barely had time to grab a toothbrush, nor did I return home that evening. Instead, Oliver rushed me down to Heathrow in his expensive Porsche, bought no doubt at the expense of his creditors, and I was on my way!

My room was not properly made up and I received an apology that night in the form of a shapely blonde with a bottle of champagne on a tray with two glasses! Even if I had such thoughts, I would never have been in a state to enjoy this little gesture! Must be a new American way of negotiating a peace offering I mused!

I met Mo at an agreed spot in the morning. For all his wealth and obvious power, I found him to be quite the most modest and kindest gentleman I had met in business. I did read recently that he had donated some twenty million dollars or more to a charity he sponsored which itself is indicative of his character. Yet he didn't flaunt his position in any way. He dressed smartly, but not to impress, and behaved like any man in the street showing the same mild manners and pleasant attitude.

My mission was to negotiate a transaction that was win-win, one in which I could offer him something in exchange for his taking an interest in our company. Asking for a mere loan, or even a partial involvement in our operation seemed meaningless for a man like him, so I took the bull by the horns and went the whole stretch. My recommendation was that he buy our company outright and use it as a back door to sell his lenses into the retail sector in the UK. Oliver remained loyal to Hoya, but if following acquisition Mo obliged the company to buy his lenses then such an acquisition would be self-financing. At the same time, he would have taken over an exciting project within Woolworths that in time would yield very handsome returns.

There was one hiccup in the negotiations once it came to his notice, I had been on the board of the company he had recently acquired. It was then he offered me a role in his enlarged group as Vice President Finance, Europe and Africa! But not only was I was no longer sure I wanted to go back into the same scenario I had left not so long before, I was also not there on personal business but working to salvage the position Oliver found himself in so I deferred any decision.

Mo sent some ex-Bausch and Lomb men around to review the situation but Brendon met them at the door and pretty much concealed any discussions from me. I was just told they only wanted to take a look around the factory operation, which of course was very much Brendon's responsibility. I should have known then he was not to be trusted, but I took him at his word and waited to hear the outcome. I will never know what he said but nothing did materialize and I never gave Mo a response to his generous offer.

And then one of those small miracles happened! Just like the television adverts at the time, a banker stepped out of the cupboard in the well-rounded shape of the man who had taken a particular interest in my progress years earlier in the commercial catering group. Given that he was ever present in those amazing years when we doubled our profits year on year our chances were suddenly looking much better. He was now looking for business through the merchant banking arm of his bank, a major player and my first employers. Our frustrated clearing bank manager had made the introduction to see if this route might produce a solution. It was like old times. We laughed that he always chose peach melba and ice cream when we lunched at the Beauport Park Hotel near Hastings. The rapport was instantly rekindled. Clifford, for want of a better name, was prepared to inject several millions into the company, but only on condition that Brendon and I took over from the family. It was his view that a "mixed board" of what he called "professionals" and "family" never worked well together. It had to be one or the other and he was not willing to finance the family! It would fall to us to ask the owners to stand down!

Wonderful, given that I had been seeking work just three months earlier when Oliver gave me employment. But how could I now be so spineless as to inform Oliver he had to move over and give me his chair! Even though this was the only available means of saving his bacon it was going to be a hard ask. I shouldn't have worried because Brendon stepped up eagerly into the role! The merchant bank advised us that a successful turnaround for the company could make us millionaires in extra short time. The bank and we two would split the shares three ways, and we would retain our shares so long as we met profit targets along the way. Fail to do so and we would have to sacrifice our shares stage by stage, but even then, we were advised the responsibilities warranted us paying ourselves a very handsome salary! We didn't need to hear any more. We were hooked!

Without fully realising it we would now be led by the nose through a myriad of obligations to be revealed only at appropriate stages, and one at a time. Had we been fully awake to this at the outset the chances are we would have thought twice. But the thought of running an independent company between us, and making a few millions in the process was a very powerful incentive. Enough you might say to turn anybody's head! We would set our own terms and conditions. My target retirement age was only three or four years away so at the very least the generous salary would get me over the finishing line! But the noose was tightening around our necks even before we got started!

We were next informed we would have to submit a business plan, and that was bread and butter work for me so caused no particular problem. Then we were informed the business plan, and much besides, would have to be audited. This was to be for the benefit of the company whom we expected would pay, but nothing prepared us for the fact we would ourselves have to pay the considerable cost if the transaction came to nothing. And we were yet to conclude negotiations with the owners who were under no obligation to agree to anything! Another noose was tightening around our necks!

Next up came the issue of security. There was never any question we would be prepared to accept a charge on our respective properties so we turned this down point blank, Brendon after some further encouragement by myself. So the bank insisted they must have some "hurt money" as they called it, the loss of which we would feel immediately if we failed. We each had to put up some £25,000 in today's terms which would be sacrificed if we failed or withdrew. That noose tightened again! We were riding a treadmill of obligations introduced in a well-rehearsed timely fashion at each point along the way! This well-oiled machine was clearly bread and butter for the merchant bank, but we were both in entirely new territory and learning as we went along! To back off at any stage would cost us increasingly more, set against the uncertainties of continuing with the mission if we did not.

Negotiations with the owners continued in earnest. One might wonder how they could possibly turn down a not inconsiderable sum, release their home from its security charge, and rid themselves of all their worries? Apparently easily! A sense of pride in the owners now took over. What was worse the coincidence of my arriving to be followed by a banking acquaintance soon after led them to believe it was all part of a prearranged plan whereby they would lose their business! No matter how hard we tried we couldn't get this notion out of Oliver's head!

Brendon remained resolute. He was of Irish descent, had those pale blue eyes, black hair, a cherub face, was softly spoken and very approachable. He adopted a concerned manner for anybody who did approach him, and immediately gained people's trust. But we had only known each other for a mere three months. No word of him had ever reached me through the industry because he had been working for a rival to my old company in Australia. The negotiations hit several impasses, but Brendon was nothing if not canny. When he told me the owner had a strong rapport with the female personnel manager, and that he intended to get close enough to use her inside knowledge I felt uneasy. Brendon carried on despite my hesitation and very soon he was in a position wherein he could use her to soften Oliver up. He was able to plant ideas and glean valuable feedback. This was all on a false promise, he confessed, that he would make her a director once we were in control! She would later regret she had ever known Brendon. Once in control he fired her and she vented her wrath by hurling a glass ash tray at his head!

After many twists and turns, the owners and ourselves met in an office in town accompanied by auditors and solicitors to conclude the buyout. All night long we thought we had negotiated a final agreement, only to find the family coming back at us time and again for fresh assurances or with fresh demands. We all finally signed up to the deal. Neither of us received a word of thanks from Oliver for having saved his bacon, and I believe to this day he is still of the mind his company was "stolen" from him!

Brendon commented on just how complex the negotiations had been to date, and I told him we had only just begun! From here on in I told him the negotiations would expand to the power of ten, and that turned out to be an understatement! Brendon was in a state of ecstasy and was fast acquiring a dangerous dose of "negotiation fever!" The immediate negotiations finally finished, we arrived back at the factory around four in the morning. We stood admiring our newly acquired company for a while and then headed off to bed. Tomorrow would see the start of a very different future.

One of the documents we signed at that epic meeting was confirmation all the information that had been offered up to the bank was, so far as we could reasonably tell, correct and truthful; that we had used "best endeavours" to ensure that this was so. It then transpired that this "best endeavours" promise had a sting in the tail. If something untoward was exposed that we might have known about, or "could" even conceivably have known about had we looked in the right place, then we would again be liable! Another noose tightening around our necks even before we had got our feet under the table!

It proved to be two years later that Clifford cheerfully told us we were "off the hook" for the specific indemnities we had been responsible for until that point! When did we sign any such indemnities!? I at least am always a very fastidious individual when it comes to signing anything. Perhaps it all seemed so routine and straightforwardly innocent at the time we never placed much significance on the matter. But it was a sharp reminder just how many different ways that proverbial noose had been tightening around our necks!

The next and final notch would be that represented by the profit targets. We were committed to hitting successive profit targets over a predetermined time scale. At each point failure to hit the targets, as mentioned, would mean we would have to sacrifice shares over to the bank, until in the end we could end up with none. Needless to say, we had no intention of missing out on our opportunity and set about the job with a relish.

Our first job was to allay fears held by our one thousand plus employees. We organised a dance to cement relations and I delivered an opening speech. Some redundancies were expected, and carried out. Not least of these was a team that Oliver kept on the payroll simply checking expense claims, a luxury we simply couldn't afford. We did as a gesture keep Oliver's ageing mother on the payroll, but in hindsight that was probably not a good idea. Meantime the personnel manager stuck rigidly to the manning formula per branch originally installed by Oliver irrespective of the level of activity, and short of firing him it was proving very hard to break old habits! All little problems to overcome along the road.

We weren't blessed with good fortunes either when a mean looking VAT man turned up to recalculate returns made under Oliver's regime. This revision cost us dearly although there was nothing wrong with the method originally used. We were staggered to learn that Customs and Excise can simply change the basis of calculation if it enhances the reward to themselves, and without any redress! As to the clearing bank, the moment our injected funds hit the account he froze the overdraft facility without notice. One might have thought the clearing and merchant bank arms of the same organisation might be working together, but seemingly this was not the case!

A year on and we proudly announced a reasonable profit, and the future was looking good. I was, as always, concerned we had all our eggs in one basket with Woolworths so I made good headway negotiating rights to set up operations in other major store groups. Woolworths were owed a considerable sum by way of arrears of license fees, which arrears had been tolerated so long as they had aspirations of converting the outstanding debt into share capital in our venture directly to themselves. But this would have seriously eroded our chances of making our fortunes, and I set about paying them off. As is often the case their line managers had not read the small print of the contract which contained the right on our side to charge them with the cost of our in-house installations. So a statement was drawn up setting our costs against the arrears. This was duly audited as provided in the contract, and the audited statement together with a much reduced cheque for the net debt owing was duly posted off to Woolworths by way of a fait accompli – one of the many ploys available to negotiators listed in chapter four.

Whilst setting about spreading our risks with other major store groups we were welcomed with open arms as our attractive looking optical installations were a marketing bonus for any store wanting to reach out to the public. But it was essential we kept any expansion to a level we could sensibly afford. However, Brendon was too easily persuaded to agree to a level of expansion that was less than cautious, and it did make me wonder if the over expansion that brought the company to its knees in the first place was the work of Brendon, and not Oliver to whom I had directed the blame in the first place!

So I had to take the reins and steer a much tighter course. As we got to know each other better I discovered Brendon had quite a religious bent, but granting him the favour of attending church with him so he could "save my soul" was not high on my priorities! Within the business his appetite for negotiating raged on unabated, and one never knew what he was negotiating or with whom, and much of my energy was spent keeping him under control.

And then the worst happened! Woolworths announced it was going to sell off all its larger High Street freeholds. With each one that closed we lost a successful business at a time when new entrants were beginning to make concerted strides into our market. Whilst our expansion into new store groups had to be curtailed competitors were not experiencing the same constraints, nor were they experiencing the loss of outlets occasioned by the Woolworth closures. Those outlets we were able to transfer elsewhere would take time to establish themselves, not least because many customers are always location loyal. We now needed a new strategy going forward to deal with the situation which was fast evolving.

It would have been natural to scale back as quickly as possible to the hard-core profits of the best branches, if only to preserve the company on a reduced scale. But at that size the fixed factory overhead would be disproportionately high, and it would be nigh on impossible to hit the profit targets set by the bank. The alternative of rebuilding the previous number of outlets to give us a chance to meet the profit targets would be fraught with liquidity problems, and the bank offered no advice. Reducing the scale of the business so dramatically would necessarily mean we would never make our millions, yet at the same time we would be placing the company in real danger again if we became too ambitious. After much debate it was agreed we would take a middle course, but at the same time divest ourselves of our factory unit. This was a valuable entity in its own right, and once divested we could still look to it to meet our needs at arm's length.

A colleague from my old plc days came to my rescue and we agreed terms for him to take over the factory unit for a very good price. The factory would remain on location which meant we would barely notice the difference, and the existing staff would be retained under the new ownership. This negotiation was beyond my wildest dreams. I even accompanied my old contact to his bank to hear from the horse's mouth that they were going to finance the transaction, a cause of action normally kept quite private to the customer! But there was a problem in the shape of the ever-active Brendon!

Whilst our future was still firmly in our own hands it then happened! In a word treason! Brendon had been flirting behind the scenes with our greatest rival who had always envied our factory facility. He had been gullible enough to believe he could stay involved with the factory unit whilst jumping ship to join our rivals. They in turn had no such intention, their only aim being to get their hands on our factory, and our position was weakened by Brendon failing to keep any confidences as to how well or otherwise we were faring at the time. Brendon's next step was to give vent to his newly found lust for negotiation by approaching Oliver, the original owner, with the suggestion he should buy back our best high street branch we still possessed in Cheltenham. This was a favourite of Oliver and suited his pride well so he made an amazingly generous offer to redeem the operation he regarded so highly. Ironically, we had put the funds in his hands to enable him to do so! Clearly Brendon didn't want to be parted from the factory operation, and these devious moves he hoped would suit his cause.

What he didn't reckon for was the moment he put these plans forward to the merchant bank our partnership was as good as over! The bank can never support such a business when the two senior partners are heading in opposite directions! In result the bank was now obliged to consider if the break-up value might be better than maintaining the company as a going concern. The price offered for the Cheltenham branch, and Brendon's smooth talking was convincing the bank that they could do very well out of selling outlets piecemeal. The more he managed to foster this image the more it appealed to the bank, but selling a practice without any fixed location was never going to be easy. Conceivably the record cards containing prescription and address details could form the basis for a new practice in the hands of budding opticians, but from my point of view this was a non-starter! Finally, there was the possibility of compensation from Woolworths for failing to meet its undertaking to maintain a minimum number of branches. Even now negotiations continued within negotiations, I would say even more so than to the power of ten I first suggested some years earlier!

In the wings our major competitor was waiting for the factory unit to fall into his lap! The longer he waited the more desperate would become our need and the better bargain he could drive, something that completely escaped both the bank and Brendon! Right at the point I had the solution in my very hands Brendon's skulduggery, and the bank's naivety, had taken it away. My period at the helm had all but seen us through the problems of being tied so closely to Woolworths that concerned me at the outset. But now the combination of the Woolworth branch closures and Brendon's treachery were causing serious harm, quite fateful in fact unless we took the route I had set out for the company. The bank couldn't be blamed, save for naively taking the wrong route out of the situation, since no bank can work with a partnership that is pulling in opposite directions. That Brendon had offered to work for half his salary showed a greater level of enthusiasm that I might have shown at the time, and this no doubt may also have steered the bank towards accepting his solution. Yet it had failure written all over it in large capital letters!

Clearly, if a breakup operation was on the cards, only one of us could remain on board to execute the plan. Since I was by now very close to my planned retirement, I threw my hat in the ring and negotiated a sensible leaving package and graciously stepped down. Brendon remained in place and twice more ran the company into the ground before the final break up was realised. None of the expectations by the bank were realised. The compensation won from Woolworths was but a token payment. No other opticians stepped forward to salvage any of the branches which had either closed or were on the point of closure. The deal I had negotiated to sell off the factory unit of course expired. Even if my former colleague had continued to express an interest it depended in turn on our remaining in situ, and retaining an ongoing interest in the premises we would be sharing. And finally, our competitor in the wings eventually picked up the factory activity at a song as I always feared he would!

My other co-directors on the trading company kicked up a fuss with the bank that Brendon had been left on board, and Clifford was soon to disappear mysteriously from the ranks of the merchant bank. Brendon never got his position he had been promised with our rival. Instead, his two fully competent underlings joined forces with our rival and Brendon, having served his purpose, was left to hang out and dry!

## Conclusion

This is a cautionary tale to warn others that mouth-watering buyout options are not always what they seem. Moreover they can be a negotiating nightmare of such ramifications you would never credit! Others following the same path will hopefully be well advised of what kind of negotiations can take place by the absorption of these pages if they are otherwise unversed with the facts. Our rare lifetime opportunity to make millions, despite being bedevilled along the way, had given me much satisfaction so there was nothing to regret. No more nooses would tighten around my neck, and it had all been worth it for the experience alone!

But it does come with a warning that "negotiation fever," can take you to places you might not want to go! Negotiations can shoot off in all directions as though they have a life of their own. You can so easily end up on that negotiating treadmill and find it no easier to get off than did Brendon. For all his devious plans Brendon was now unemployed, and far from retirement, at his own hand! Whilst we never made our millions you could say we were never bored, to say the least!

## Brendon

With Brendon's participation in the company finally at an end he joined the clergy of which he was so fond. When I opened my local paper, and saw his cherub face peering up in full religious regalia, I had to take a second look! There he was preaching the gospel to all who would listen if only they knew! But little did they! First a college confided in me Brendon had borrowed a significant sum from him, raised through his own mother, that he never saw again. A year or so still later I nearly fell off my chair when there was that same cherub face adorning the same paper! This time he had persuaded a frail parishioner to appoint him as his enduring power of attorney. A relative first raised suspicions, and it was eventually discovered Brendon had financed his daughter's wedding out of the man's estate, and much more besides. All in all, at least £150,000 had been filched in today's values. The judge declared that, had Brendon not been challenged, he would have disposed of his victim's entire estate. He was duly sentenced to three years in jail and that was the last I heard of him.

**Key Tactics Summary**

Never finance a business on short term overdrafts.

When you acquire a family concern don't retain staff entrenched in the old ways.

Be proactive in selling a solution to a problem.

Look for that win-win situation.

Know what you are getting into.

Know who you are "getting into bed" with.

Don't be hoodwinked.

Beware the over enthusiastic amateur negotiator!

Don't see things at face value.

Be fully aware of your liability for costs and risks up front.

Anticipate your opposite number's position and his thinking.

You may gleam much by chatting to his associates.

Always trust your judgement.

Put a brake on runaway negotiation fever.

Don't be oblivious to "treason"

Think twice before you act ruthlessly.

Ashtrays can be dangerous!

# Chapter 26
# At the Royal Court

I should say at the outset that this is a play on the word "court" since royalty was involved, but the court in question was a badminton court! A position as chief executive of the Badminton Association, England and Wales was vacant and I was one of a substantial number who applied for the position. Because the right candidate would have the full responsibility of organising the national team for the world championships in Jakarta, and also the Olympics, the negotiating committee had to be certain of their appointee. Furthermore, the appointee would be liaising regularly with the patron who was a senior member of the Royal Family, so the interview arrangements were quite extraordinary. Never before or since have I negotiated a job with personnel that went to such extreme lengths.

Those conducting the interviews included the chairman, the present incumbent, a professional recruitment officer and three or four others with strong connections to the Association. It was a position that appealed to me because I had always been a keen sportsman and it seemed a dream opportunity to be paid for work that would be as much a pleasure as an obligation. I was very much aware that my chess captain, Baruch Wood, made his living out of chess and I always envied him his position. I attended two interviews in front of the keen eyes and ears of the entire selection team. Then I was recalled for a day going through personality and intelligence tests. Next followed a further interview when I was informed of the result of the tests and cross examined on my attitude towards them. Then a further interview with the chairman, who seemed to resent the fact that my car, a leftover from my previous job, was more expensive than his. Having lived in the Midlands, a prime centre for car manufacture for some years, I was well aware of the aura with which cars were regarded. As soon as you shook hands with a stranger the subject seemed to revert immediately to the car you were driving. It was all a strange kind of snobbery of which the retiring chairman had a big dose! I would not be awarded such a car by the Association, he eagerly asserted, but then who needed a car when a fine house was provided along with the job!? At the next interview those present reverted to the full number again. It seemed to me during the course of the interview they were playing a ruse to see if I could be trusted in the company of young fit sports women. A shapely young woman in sporting gear flitted back and forth past the open door in full view, all too obviously so, so I steeled my eyes away! That done I and the top seven candidates moved into a boardroom where we were each asked in turn to assume the role of chairman. A subject was dropped in our laps, more often than not a controversial one, and we had the task of leading the others through a debate over the matter. In the case of smoking could we, for example, be seen taking contributions from a cigarette manufacturer, and so on.

Each of us took it in turn. When it came to my turn, I let the debate continue for a while, and then decided I would declare a personal interest before purporting to take a vote. Regrets were expressed that I had not let the debate go on longer, but then I never did enjoy playing charades! We were all cross examined next as to how we felt the other candidates had performed. One such candidate had decided to take a very aggressive attitude against the rest of us which I felt would hardly fit the requirements for diplomacy. However, in due course I was astonished to hear he was offered the job, but declined. Perhaps he was a plant to test our assessment capabilities, one would never know. In the event two of us were then placed on the final short list. The chief executive of the table tennis association of England and Wales didn't make the cut when I thought he at least had appropriate experience.

Great emphasis was placed on my readiness and commitment to lead the team through the world championships and the Olympic games, both within the next eighteen months. I was questioned how I would get on with the patron and my views of the royal family. If I got the job, they asked, how would I make myself known to him. I replied I would simply phone his secretary, tell her I had been appointed and hold myself available to meet the royal patron at his convenience. That went down well. It was also revealed that the queen herself turned up at the badminton centre from time to time and took a strong interest, so I would be responsible for entertaining her on such occasions.

To facilitate the final selection one George and I were to present ourselves at the private home of the chairman on a pleasant Sunday. We were to dress casual smart and George had the morning, and I the afternoon. What I had in my favour were my general management skills and first-hand participation in sport, so I would know what made our national players tick you could say, and also earn their respect. George was plump and more rounded, had a rich public schoolboy plummy voice, and a jovial personality. I certainly couldn't see him rushing around a badminton court, nor establishing much of a rapport with seasoned athletes either!

The incumbent chief executive made no bones of the fact he supported myself, and I rather suspect he took a bit of a dim view of the outgoing chairman, as did I. As it happened, I had also been invited to spend some more time with the chairman earlier in the process to give me a second opportunity to impress, but he still seemed to be having difficulty overcoming the spectacle of my car! The mere knowledge I had evidently not impressed him over much the first time around made it all the more difficult for me to find the right words!

The Sunday afternoon came around and I duly arrived at the chairman's house to be greeted by the party, now reduced to some three or four. The discussions centred on how well or otherwise I thought I had done. Key aspects of all the previous discussions were touched on wherever points needed clarification. On entering the lounge, I did quite innocently commit a rather unfortunate faux pas. There on the mantlepiece was a picture of Sir George Andrew Thomas, one-time English chess champion, and the founder and patron of the Badminton Association itself. I blurted out that he had "introduced himself to me" back in my days in junior chess tournaments, which was perfectly true as he did take pains to introduce himself to budding players, but it came out as though I were the dignitary and he the one pleased to know me! Ouch! When asked if there was anything I regretted I referred immediately to that instant, but never really felt the chairman was fully satisfied! Not my best piece of negotiating unfortunately!

We had reached the final leg of the ordeal. I was told to step out into the garden along with the professional recruiting representative for a concluding chat. Once there he confided in me the committee were split equally down the middle. He had the deciding vote and the job was mine if I could convince him in the next half hour I wouldn't disappear the moment the next senior job was offered me in industry! I learned a valuable lesson here in that I should have immediately had my speech prepared and gone in hard in favour of the appointment. But I did have a conscience about not misleading them, and at the back of my mind I considered for a moment what it would mean in terms of seeing my children, having not long divorced. The distance alone represented a major problem, and not least when I would be required to do a fair degree of globetrotting.

I could have made it clear I not only wanted the appointment, but was about to imminently step down from my current position, but mistakenly hesitated for fear of any inferences that might be drawn from that.

At that moment the job was as good as in my hands when a shout came from the direction of the house. We had been cautioned that the wife of the chairman was ill and we may have to call the meeting off at short notice, and that was exactly what had happened even before I could get a word out of my mouth! Either that or the chairman had talked one of the committee around to his preferred choice!

In the event it was George who got the call later that evening and I was informed of the decision. On reflection I did feel more relieved than disappointed, but it certainly was a once in a lifetime opportunity. As job negotiations go this one exceeded all expectations and lessons might be drawn from this experience.

I have been involved in some rather strange interview positions in general. In one situation wherein I had already been employed for a number of years I was invited to attend an interview to be given the "once over" for a promotion. I mused how anybody considered a stranger would know me better than the colleagues I had worked with for years! It seemed they had fallen in favour with some American style psychological torture! And on another occasion just such an American interviewer was dispatched to make my casual acquaintance in my local pub of all places! It was only when his questions seemed too pertinent to my position I guessed he had been planted! Some organisations love to use such demeaning interview techniques so be careful!

**Key Tactics Summary**

Telling the truth can be the best option.

Do so with confidence.

Be alert to underhand techniques.

Don't submit to the psychological interview fad.

Know yourself and your own mind as soon as possible.

Hesitation has consequences.

Don't glance sideways at any attractive young ladies during the interview process.

# Chapter 27
# Dealing with Demigods

The board room is usually the focus for discussion, debate and determination of all matters crucial to an organisation.

There are usually opposite and diverse opinions as to which way to proceed on all manner of things. The discussions that precede these important decisions can be regarded as internal negotiations between conflicting options. Those participating will be skilled in negotiating as in all other such environments. Demigods have an insatiable appetite as a rule for power. As such they can dictate or stifle open discussion, and unless you act in consult there is always risk as they hold your future in their hands. They will act as though they own you, and manipulate you at will if you permit them.

Once when I was quite settled in a position, I needed confirmation of a pending increase in salary with which to justify a mortgage for a property I was anxious to make my home. My simple request was quashed from above because I was being eyed up for promotion, and my private wishes were not going to be allowed to take precedence at any cost! In the circumstances there was little or nothing I could do about the situation, and in time I was offered and accepted the challenge of the promotion. But I always resented the presumption that the demigod at the helm could dictate life events in such a manner!

So how do they accomplish this grand position of power?

Firstly, by showing a ruthless streak. In one company some sixty directors came and went worldwide in my time, not all but I would say a great many at the hands of the top man. The power to sack is all too often used like a drug to the worst of their number. They are masters of the put down. At the time when I was being elevated to replace a colleague the top man placed a book I had written on the outgoing executive's desk, and that days before he was about to be dismissed! It was a mean trick to no doubt demean him and in some way support the rationale for my promotion in his place. When he thanked me for the book that had appeared on his desk, I was placed in a very difficult position of explaining it was not I that had placed it there!

Demigods seldom give encouragement or show gratitude. More commonly they are ultra-critical and always claim the high ground for themselves. They take all the credit going to themselves, earned or otherwise, but never fail to look for scapegoats if things go awry. They negotiate and manoeuvre themselves into unassailable towers of strength over time, and they are not beyond climbing up on the backs of others. They will then consolidate their position by the management structures they build around themselves. These are intended to stifle honest internal negotiations and give them the final word in all things.

So what kind of structures lend themselves to this approach? A typical ploy is the use of non-executive directors. Much can be said for the advantage of having a pool of experienced directors on the board from other companies or positions. They have no direct executive responsibilities but recognise situations when they occur from their own experience and can contribute from their extensive knowledge. That said the ones so often appointed are close colleagues of the top man, and their appointment is seen by him as a source of support and loyalty in all circumstances. So if the demigod wishes to push through a certain policy with the executive, he merely has to report that it is the will of the holding board! In truth he might well have presented the policy to the holding board himself as though it were the will of the executive! Neither body really has the facts before them as to who genuinely supported which cause of action, nor even what the considerations were. That is with the sole exception of a minority of key executive directors the demigod trusts and invites to join him on the holdings board. Failure to support him at all times and they will be shown the door.

Executives eager for recognition will be given directorships on the trading company boards, but that will mean nothing if the only meetings held at that level are for statutory purposes, such as the annual general meeting. However, there will be an executive committee next under the formal structures to which will be appointed the key managers that run the business day to day. The top man will chair these meetings, perhaps with the support of other trusted colleagues alongside, and this body will be treated more or less as a progress chasing operation in which instructions are given down and pressure exerted. Lip service is paid to any consideration of democracy. The structure described enables a demigod, even at the head of a public company accountable to shareholders, to get away with virtually sole control. In fact, it is largely in such public companies that we find this kind of structure because in smaller private companies it is usually well known that the owners have the whip hand without all the pretence. Everything is set up for the sake of appearances, but look a little deeper and you will see the truth is far different.

On joining such an organisation, I was briefed by a colleague once that you "only speak if invited!" We were all expected to follow the prompts or instructions of the chief executive or otherwise remain silent, something I was quite unable to comply with but survived by cautiously negotiating my way into a strong position, and not least with the banks, when many others fell under the sword.

Demigods will feel no shame in giving themselves perks or advantages as they regard them as their sovereign right. They feel that they can do whatever they like at any time. They might stop off in the middle of a business trip to take a few days holiday in the sun, and think nothing of it, but deny the same advantages to others. Demigods will not see their directors as equal partners, and you will never feel the same by a large margin. As a director you will be afraid to make any significant decisions without first referring to them, more especially so in private companies. This not only blunts your effectiveness but will be seen as such by executives further down the pecking order. You will not only be less effective but will lose respect amongst the more junior managers, and the business suffers in result.

It was in such a private company already referred to when the managing director purported to tell me what the profit was going to be before I had even embarked upon the task of preparing the accounts! And an attempt was made to make it clear my job depended upon my delivering what was required! If this all sounds grossly exaggerated or inaccurate that is because it only happens in the hands of demigods, as they think of themselves, who behave so atrociously

With the erosion of time operations run by demigods find themselves lacking in quality of management in depth.

They fail to bring other executives on, and they never relinquish their power base. As they age, they become dangerously set in their ways, do not keep abreast of new developments, and stick to old methods despite the world moving on. Many only found their seat of power through a series of acquisitions in the first place, which is not as honourable as building up their empires from scratch. In the end their group grows so large it is crying out for decentralisation but this is denied, and they grow more distant and out of touch. Show disloyalty and you are shown the door. Hint at leaving and they will bear a grudge against you for the rest of your time, irrespective of whatever circumstances prompted you in the first place.

The minds of demigods become ever more inflexible as time goes by, and the company will suffer accordingly. They will try to demonstrate their hold of matters by constantly quoting out of date facts and figures as their mantra. Sacred cows will be challenged over your dead body so to speak.


Depressing as the foregoing sounds there are surely as many chief executives who operate in a far more equitable manner, and of these I recall that my old chairman G C D'Arcy Biss was the exact antithesis of this characterisation. He was a Churchillian type of figure. He always insisted on Romeo and Juliet, Havana Cigars, and always wore a white carnation in his buttonhole. He was very broad and had a shock of white hair and a reddened face. When it came to handling discrete negotiations he showed much to be admired.

I remember years ago we conducted a minor "negotiation" between ourselves over our conflicting headwear. Bowler hats were still the fashion in the city but I was walking down Threadneedle Street towards the Bank of England side by side with D'Arcy, myself sporting a Frank Sinatra hat with a feather in it as against his bowler! Feeling I had to say something I ventured to comment we made "a fine pair" walking along in our different headwear. Without as much as looking up, his cigar protruding out of his mouth, he said in that deep plummy voice,

*"Yes, get a bowler!"*

Being a generation younger it really wasn't my style and never happened but his remark, and the manner of if, still amuses me to this day.

I also found D'Arcy very endearing on the occasion of one of our AGM's. It was a running joke that we would normally finish our AGM in little over two minutes and then shuttle off to lunch. But one year three individuals, each with a grudge, had made it known they would be putting us to the sword. The first was the main auditor amongst some fifteen separate auditing firms around the group. We wanted to rationalise with one prominent audit firm to cover the entire group, and he was there to argue we should give him the entire responsibility. The second was touting for business claiming to be an expert at reducing stock levels, and he was right on the money! And the third was a disgruntled credit controller who had been dismissed, and was only entitled to attend by virtue of a few shares awarded under a share incentive scheme. His ethnic routes were Indian and, having never met him, I knew nothing more than that about him. But the expectation was he could be very disruptive and was not going to be easily silenced.

Negotiating tactics were discussed beforehand and we decided simply to give him enough rope to hang himself, to coin a phrase. We would not at any cost enter any form of discussion of any kind with him. The meeting commenced and all three tried to speak over each other, but D'Arcy restored some order and we dealt with the question of the audit and the stock expert with due consideration.

And then came the disgruntled ex-employee. He started off very eloquently and I was almost beginning to believe him myself. He most certainly had the ears of the other shareholders present which was a somewhat disarming situation. But the longer he spoke the greater the rage he worked himself into. All this time nobody made any comment to anything that was said, as prearranged. His ranting was focused on making critical comments as opposed to asking questions which might ordinarily have drawn a response. Finally, he ran out of material and made one last startling threat.

*"If you don't comply,"*

he ranted,

*"I'll fast to the death."*

The moment had finally arrived and D'Arcy to his undying credit looked over his half-rimmed gold spectacles, flicked the ash of his cigar, and merely grunted,

*"Thank you!"*

It was the perfect response D'Arcy had been waiting to utter.

The complainant had lost all credibility and we cheerfully made our way to lunch along with our invited guests, all with a large grin spreading over their faces.

They were in fact the first and the last words uttered by D'Arcy throughout the ordeal who played the situation like the experienced expert he was. Just shows how a little preparation goes a long way.

**Key Tactics Summary**

Know how a company is set up before joining them.

Know how they think and what makes them tick.

Be careful you are not being used.

Sharpen your skills in dealing with industrial bullies.

Plan ahead to deal with disruptive malcontents.

If you have responsibilities then refuse to be silenced.

Being brave may be the only way to protect your own legal position at the hands of demigods.

# Chapter 28
# The Hit Squad

The very antitheses of negotiation was exercised by the "hit squad" employed by one of the most successful public groups in the country. In fact, this is the only example in this work of a total void in negotiation, even worse than that exercised by demigods. If you see this in your organisation you may be in for a very rough ride!

The group, since broken up, used to turn badly performing companies around and ensure that in time they recorded super profits. Any drop in performance and the directors would be looking over their shoulders for the first sign of the infamous "hit squad". This would be represented by a convey of black BMW's coming through the gates, and a bunch of smug aggressive individuals arriving at the door under the enthusiastic authority of the top man. Such was their intent on fostering this image that any executive parking a black BMW outside the plant would face consequences! I was informed that my rather handsome Jaguar would be severely frowned upon if seen on the premises, so I had to step down to my trusted old Ford Estate. It was that Midlands "car" status rearing its ugly head all over again!

One of the most successful of its subsidiary companies was a provider of components to the motor industry, and I found myself there in my role as a consultant. Before long we received the bad news that the Ford Motor Company had decided to take the production of the Ford Sierra seats in-house. The company also made the facias for the Jaguar and Land Rover range, parts for trucks and various other supplies to the industry at large. It was a very successful company making just the kind of super profits the group demanded, but it was immediately clear that, in the absence of the Sierra seat, the profit level would be handsome but not up to the normal high expectations.

It was decided to hive the company off as it no longer brought any excitement to the group, or fitted their investment profile. In the absence of a managing director designated specifically to the company, and a finance director, it was felt that any potential buyer would be discouraged. In result I was invited to take a directorship until such time as the operation could be offloaded. But efforts failed in the short term and before we as much as drew breath, we were faced with that fearsome spectacle of the fleet of black BMW's coming through the gates! For maximum impact there was never any advanced warning, they simply appeared and immediately ruled the roost!

In all my experience the first thing you would do when such an announcement as that made by Ford was on the table would be to call a meeting of directors. You would assess the situation and determine which strategy to follow. But the board consisting of myself, a production director, research and sales directors, and with the input of the sub-group managing director were not for a second given their heads. It was as though none of us actually existed.

Perhaps the hit squad had a particular expertise which the local management never could, or maybe they were without a project and we drew the short straw. But then in such circumstances the local board were always discounted in favour of using the bullying hit squad who were well versed in sorting out such problems. Either way in they came with that exaggerated swagger! There was to be no negotiation of any kind. The senior member was repugnant. He was arrogant beyond imagination. The subgroup managing director accompanied him into my office, from which point he was all the more abrasive to him and also myself. Demanding to know what experience I had he listened to about four words, and immediately scoffed at the response. The group MD tried to intervene and defend his position in the company, but was shown the door. When he protested our little Hitler only had to make as though he was reaching for the phone to talk to Mr. Big, who became a very famous industrialist, when my new colleague saw the point and disappeared off the premises never to return!

Much was made of any paperwork on my desk. I was told my nasty little visitor "Didn't like to see paperwork on any surface". It all had to be dust free and shiny. It was as though I had somehow been magically transported back to my army days. Given the choice I am sure I would sooner have been back in khaki. I immediately wrote my resignation letter and confided as much to my colleagues who encouraged me to hold my horses. It was common knowledge that when the hit squad cleared out the old management, they were quite generous with compensation payments they informed me. On the last leg of my journey to early retirement I have to admit this did appeal and, for the moment at least, I swallowed my pride.

The modus operandi of the hit squad was consistently to reorganise any operation from top to bottom, either in order to restore super profits or to offload it once the first objective was achieved. From that point on anybody they retained was there only to do their bidding. All but myself and the research director were shown the door in the traditional fashion the next day. It was understood within the group that as soon as you saw those black BMW's the incumbent directors would all be gone before the end of the day! Just the two of us now remained. Junior managers and staff with weak constitutions staggered out before they were dismissed. Any our fierce friend had a use for were offered attractive compensation inducements to retain them. Some accepted if they were unlikely to get employment elsewhere, something the tyrant would no doubt already have taken into account.

Most rational executives would be anxious to retain those offering special skills and experience, but it was as though the world had been turned upside down. People were dispensed with relish and cast aside. It was all part of a well-oiled system of tearing down, and then building up the organisation in the desired image. It was doubted any senior management would survive such an ordeal so a new team was always being groomed behind the scenes to succeed them. No shame or pretext was made of this whatever and it was apparently the way the group operated consistently!

The bully's attempt to humiliate all and sundry continued day after day unabated. Any activities carrying lower returns were weeded out, as were any underused physical areas of the factory and offices. The objective was to see how much of the profitable business could be squeezed into a smaller unit to maximise results. Any line eliminated would be run around the clock to raise stock levels immediately prior to discontinuation. This was a case when prices for the product would be raised substantially, and customers given a short period to bolster their supplies before production halted completely. In doing so chemicals poured out at dangerous levels and I had to call in the Health and Safety officers. They were given short shrift and shown the door without achieving anything.

I agreed to remain in place to help with the operation for up to fifteen months. My natural obstinacy held my head in the air despite the occasional flare up between us, and the time ticked away. As it did so I kept my eye on the Footsie share index. The actions of Margaret Thatcher led to interest rates as high as nineteen per cent or more. Whilst this was crippling all but the most efficient firms, it served to diminish the power of the unions. In the midst of such mayhem stock market values acted in quite the reverse manner one would expect. Just when companies were folding everywhere share values were going up in anticipation of better times, and not falling as one would suppose. And the highest ever interest rates were pulling annuity rates to a similar high.

Taken together I didn't miss the fact it would be the best opportunity in my lifetime to convert my pension fund into an annual annuity, thus giving me both security and my freedom to retire early. If I missed the opportunity now, I might never see the same again. I would end up in the years to come working for next to nothing over and above the pension I might have received. And the good news was I could secure a pension contract up to one year ahead without drawing it down until I retired!

Now it was a case of watching the days expire hoping that the day my services were no longer required would coincide with the date I was due to drawdown my first pension payment! The deal I got was just about the best that could be obtained since I had always engendered the best of relationships with my brokers. They in turn explored the entire annuity market to get best value for money, when I hadn't given much thought to the notion you might shop around for annuities. Even an innocent enough medical condition could enhance the rate of annuity you obtained beyond all expectations. The choice of indexation was of paramount importance, but my judgement turned out to be sound over time.

Time elapsed, and right on cue the tyrant came into my office to inform me, *"It was time to go home!"*

A less qualified individual was apparently now ready and the business was going to be transformed into a "man and a dog" operation he informed me. I feigned disappointment as best I could, took the cheque, and was last seen running as fast as my legs would carry me! My pension deal was the best negotiation I ever conducted, and which I might well have missed had I not been sharp enough to see the possibilities. Now at the early age of fifty I was free to follow other pursuits. Now for that last marathon, and then the world!

**Key Tactics Summary**

For many reasons knowing how a company is run is a valuable insight if you can discover the facts.

Stand your ground if they are trying to use you.

Dealing with industrial bullies requires a certain attitude and particular technique.

Be every ready to negotiate.

If you are caught by surprise play for time.

End of production line price hikes can give high yields.

Don't miss the obvious opportunity.

Always research your options.

Know that goodwill is part of your negotiation armoury.

# Chapter 29
# In the Written Form

Throughout the book no distinction has been made in the negotiating process between cases completed verbally or those in written form. It is clear from many of the examples that for the most part verbal exchanges are assumed. However, there are lessons to be learned here. To begin with some people are better at one or the other, and it is always good advice to play to your strengths, something that also applies to particular techniques or tactics employed.

Negotiating partly or wholly in the written form does have particular advantages and disadvantages. The most obvious disadvantage is that you are unable to convey extra meaning or emphasis through facial expressions and the pitch of your voice, but then neither are you so likely to give your position away. On the other hand, a major advantage of the written negotiation is that the indisputable evidence of what has been said and agreed is there permanently for all to see, much in the same way as the notes or minutes of agreements were strongly recommended to consolidate your position in an earlier chapter. It was the carefully maintained coverage in writing of the events leading up to the high court case in chapter thirteen that saved the day. They provided undisputed evidence that the author had taken appropriate steps to circumvent the problems created through seagulls scavenging the rubbish. In the absence of this record the outcome would most certainly have been very much at risk. This is a good example of how the written word can be far more powerful than the spoken.

For every example given in this book of a successful verbal negotiation the author is aware of at least an equal number over the years which were entirely conducted in written form. The modern era has made this so very much easier.

With the advent of technology, and especially computers, few people send handwritten letters these days. A computer produced message, report or letter, can easily be corrected for grammatical or spelling errors. Moreover, if you have second thoughts on a section it can be instantly deleted or amended. As a principle I more often than not create a draft in the first instance and refrain from dispatching it by whichever method until the next day. I never fail to be amazed at the way the mind works during sleeping hours as I frequently wake conscious of desirable amendments or even a quite different approach in my mind as to what I might have said. Anything too aggressive can be wrinkled out; points not emphasized enough can be strengthened; important omissions can be introduced after a thorough reappraisal of what you have written. Often times I find myself waking in the small hours of the morning, my brain exercised in the semi-conscious state writing or rewriting the very letter almost without me if that makes sense. By the time you have experienced what difference it can make by creating a draft first and reviewing it the next day you will use this method whenever possible, and I fully recommend it to you. I'm sure that if you do not already adopt this practice you will not fail but be surprised at the benefit it gives you. It is quite a phenomenon the manner in which the brain continues to work whilst you are asleep, but do remember that in some folk this can be rather disturbing to the sleep pattern. There is no greater example of this than when, for example, writing a long report or a work such as this. The author is often disturbed by a constant stream of fresh ideas invading his sleep, and sometimes in stark contrast to the mind sketching out a simple communication he finds himself writing whole chapters, and not always what was intended or in any way useful! Suffice to say that once such a task is complete this mental process thankfully declines unless and until another such venture is taken on.

Probably the most regular use of the written form is when you find yourselves in some form of dispute. You are far less likely to go into written negotiation mode, for example, if you were selling a property. In the first instance somebody, not necessarily yourself, has to show interested parties around. It is then practical and expedient to field all the questions and answers on the spot verbally. To attempt to deal with all the myriad questions and answers one at a time in written form would take forever and be most impracticable. So using the written form of negotiation you are far more likely to be trying to protect your rights on some matter, perhaps with local authorities. Or you may be seeking to claim compensation for example from a services company, or in regard to a failed product or an inadequate repair job.

In such cases you will want, above all things, to write a good letter marshalling all the relevant arguments and expressing yourself well. Always read your drafted letter carefully through. As the threads of your argument spring

191

to mind jot them down initially on a scrap of paper before you commence writing. We are all aware that others will most probably occur to you as you write, and if you give yourself time before concluding your communication you will be less disappointed that you have left important points out. Take pains not to be verbose. Keep the communication as short as possible if you want it to have maximum impact. People soon tire of reading over long scripts, and the essential points escape the mind in its reading if they are buried in a lot of unnecessary language.

In a complex case, or when there are many separate points to be made a longer script is sometimes unavoidable. Even then if you read through a few times, it is usually possible to shorten it significantly without losing meaning.

Excellence comes with practice and experience. Your communication will benefit enormously if you weed out any inappropriate aggressive comments or assertions. Clumsy spelling errors, even if irrelevant to the point in issue, will let you down and even detract from the regard the recipient has of you. If in doubt just use a spell check or a dictionary app which almost all computers have these days as a matter of course. The better your letter in all respects the greater will be its impact, so it is wise to constantly sharpen your writing skills and be conscious of the benefits that come with that extra effort.

There are some forms of negotiation for which the written form is the only one possible. Say you are complaining to British Gas or some other supplier for terrible service. You may try and argue the matter over the phone but there is no chance whatever they will consider the matter until they receive a written complaint. The author encountered just such a situation quite recently when a service engineer failed to attend a pre booked annual service appointment. This appointment was in regard to a holiday home in Cornwall which had been booked to coincide with a break the author had planned for himself in this property on the coast. Various computer-generated messages informed him that the service engineer would be "arriving on a certain date," that "he was on his way", "that he would arrive at a certain time," and finally that "due to pressure of demand your appointment has been cancelled", and "phone this number and make a new appointment", end of!

After having waited in for half a frustrating day the author was none too pleased, and even less so when he phoned the number advised only to find all the options led him nowhere until after quite some time the call was finally closed down. Furthermore, no alternative appointments were then available before he had to return home, even had he been able to speak to anybody!

The trip would have been made just the same were it not for the appointment, but the failure of the service engineer to arrive could only mean another journey down to Cornwall necessitating another round trip of some five hundred miles at a future date, not necessarily when it was convenient.

So the author felt fully justified in using a bit of poetic license and emphasizing all the trouble and expense he had gone to in his letter of complaint that followed, not to mention all the inconvenience. A monetary sum was claimed for the cost of travel, and an apology was requested since something of the same kind had happened on a previous occasion already. The gas board advised him it was granted two months by law in which to consider any claim for compensation; two months during which the service would remain unfulfilled and no liability admitted! During this time the service contract was due for its annual renewal but whilst the matter was in abeyance the author had no appetite for paying further sums for another year. That decision produced a response to the effect that the contract was now cancelled, and before the boiler could be taken back onto a new contract it would have to be examined for efficiency. If it was not found to be up to a certain standing there was no guarantee it would be accepted onto contract! Even then we were informed it would be at the current higher market price!

Difficult self-defeating telephone conversations followed and it was time to bring together all the pertinent lines of argument in a carefully prepared letter.

Quantified and other demands were made in respect of the following:-

1. Full travel expenses to the location and back.
2. Refund for the service not carried out.
3. The service be carried out as a matter of urgency.
4. A new contract to be issued at a competitive price.
5. Compensation for all the inconvenience.
6. An apology.

The offer received fell short of expectations and came with the suggestion that, were this not to be acceptable, then "an appeal could be made to the Ombudsman". No apology of any kind was offered and it was asserted that the matter of our inconvenience was not one that could be considered. So I did exactly what they suggested and approached the Ombudsman. The finally negotiated package amounted to some three hundred and fifty pounds, but the Ombudsman insisted on a further one hundred for the inconvenience caused. And by the time it had all been settled time had elapsed without incident effectively saving a further subscription for the next year. The new subscription was competitive, and there was no assertion the boiler was inadequate despite its advancing years.

In summary it was the marshalling together of all available points of argument, and their expression in a cogent well drafted communication beyond dispute that finally won the day. One of those examples when the author sensed that he was about to turn a disaster into a profit!

Issues related to Planning permission are another area where they can only proceed to a certain point by verbal communication, and where the authorities will insist on your putting your case in writing.

The author lived at one point in a grade two listed property in a conservation area bordering a rather pleasant courtyard which had won various "Best of Britain" awards over the years. A management company had been run by two directors and a company secretary who carried out most of the administrative functions necessary for the efficient running of operations. It served the needs of fifteen properties all in all. Over the years the lead director (we will call him "Tony") successfully saw that the very attractive courtyard area should be regarded as sacrosanct; that it should remain intact free of any development of any kind. This was fully supported and in result the courtyard was not in any way changed for some thirty years. No individual member could thus put forward a project, however small, for his own benefit that would impinge on the amenity of somebody else. Nobody asked and nobody got, and nobody suffered any disturbance, anxiety or heartache.

The company secretary was a new arrival and it was he who had ambitions to extend his property from a doorway to accommodate a toilet and shower. For the first time in several decades owners had to face a request that interrupted a minor but pleasant right of way, at the same time detracting from the open view of greenery from the location opposite. It was never going to be easy as the individual concerned was in a fiduciary position and did much work for the community. Whilst the request was voted down it was conceded that a small porch roof over the door could be tolerated. That was the signal for the foot-in-the-door opportunity the individual concerned was going to exploit to the full! What followed was an object lesson in negotiation by chiselling away, by one means or another, at the status quo until all objections would be finally overcome.

Individuals who needed to be approached were spoken to in turn in an effort to "soften them up." Next the issue was brought up at an annual meeting wherein it was argued the company should have some formal guidelines written into the rules governing such matters. The secretary put forward the basis on which he recommended such rules could be introduced and they were adopted. Of course he knew well what he was doing, and it was a meeting the writer could not as it happened attend. As a rather clever but well thought out move the rules he recommended were such that his previous proposal, which had been turned down, would stand up well against them. And of course no provision in these rules said anything about rights of way which would have given grounds for objection! As a matter of fact he denied the right of way existed as such since it ran into an area of common land that had already been absorbed as "his garden," this in turn being justified by a claim he "maintained it!" Of course presuming to maintain an area does not in any confer ownership, but he was a smooth operator and made inroads whilst the remainder simply did nothing for the sake of peace – or on the other hand through sheer indifference if it had no impact on themselves.

With such an important change to the company rules the best practice would have been to make the intention known within the agenda circulated ahead of the meeting. The author for one would certainly have gone to extra lengths to attend had he had prior notice yet, as another clever negotiating sleight of hand, the issue was brought up under "any other business".

One wonders if anybody really knew what was happening when the new rules were duly adopted. The new rules themselves stated that any future applications would be judged against the following criteria:-

1. The impact it might have generally on other residents.
2. The effect on adjacent properties.
3. How it would affect the beauty and aesthetics of the courtyard.
4. Whether the size and proportionality was in keeping with maintaining the ethos and atmosphere.
5. Whether it would conform to the agreed aims and objectives of the company.
6. Whether it met conservation and listed building planning rules.

It only fell for the secretary to present anew the same application that had been previously voted out and this time it would have been all the more difficult to argue against it!

But it appears he was sufficiently aware of the pitfalls of attempting this that he elected to skip that step altogether.

Given that the new rules (introduced by himself) would appear to be supportive of his case, he could now argue that the shareholders had by voting the rules in accepted his application by implication! A vote would no longer be necessary providing he could get the support of the directors – a far easier task since he was working with them on a regular basis. In lieu of a meeting members were consulted on a one-by-one basis thus eliminating any negative discussion on the proposal. No general discussion was afforded in meeting. Somewhere in the process it had been argued that the relatively small development would make the property more appealing, and thus add to the general appearance of the courtyard, so it would seem that became the fallback position.

I could see that the director that had effectively vetoed any such development over the years was likely to continue his opposition, and with only two directors that would halt his progress. So the Secretary set about befriending a member of the courtyard that had similar interests to himself, and lo and behold it was not long before he was recommended and appointed an additional director. Now he could rely upon a majority of directors so far as their number was concerned.

Within the year the building commenced. Anybody looking in from outside would fail to understand how a majority of fifteen owners had first voted against the project yet here it was in the making with little further ado. It had proved an object lesson in how a combination of clever manoeuvring and persistence, each hindrance overcome at a time, finally succeeded.

The time came and the new director, we will call him Paul, became brave enough to put forward his own proposals for a small extension on the ground level. Once again it would have to be agreed that a small parcel of community land be sold to him for the purpose. However this time it blocked an important view and potentially spoiled the amenity of the author.

A planning application had been made discretely by Paul without as much as referring the matter to the directors, let alone other members. Since Paul's particular property was not listed it was pretty obvious the application would be granted at the outset. Planning rules turn a completely blind eye to the protection of views, and providing their light meters record a sufficient amount of light such an application is likely to succeed. The author based his objection to Planning on the despoiling of the general amenity, the disfiguring of the attractive old fashioned courtyard, his loss of views and light. Naming the loss of light was a grave error because when it was outrightly rejected by Planning it created a weak spot in the author's case even though the Planning department rules did not carry the same scope as those of the management company

The author got his objections into Planning as quickly as possible in the hope this would clinch the matter before a decision was called for by the directors of the management company. But, knowing in his heart this was likely to fail, he turned his attention to how he might win the directors and other members over to his point of view. This was best done in writing so that nobody could conveniently overlook what had been argued and conceded when the "old boys act" of the ruling cliche got themselves involved. What now should the writer do to further    defend his interests!? First and foremost all communications he decided would be in writing as suggested above. He would create a paper trail setting out each line of argument and their responses up to the point a decision was made.

First things first. Paul had been presumptuous enough to make a planning application without first making his intentions known to anybody on site. His ally the secretary must have given him the nod to take this action for him to invest in a surveyor and planning fees upfront, the author concluded. As for the author he had had the advantage of prior knowledge having seen a builder and surveyor on site measuring up ahead of the application.

The first message by email was addressed to the Secretary asking him if he was aware of this activity, the intention being to firstly discover the facts but secondly to set the cat amongst the pigeons by making it known Paul had been so presumptuous. By the polite response received it became clear that this much had been accomplished. The author's message and the response are both copied below

*Hi (Secretary)*

*There seems to be quite a lot of activity on the corner of Paul's house suggestive of some kind of development onto community land. which we have always treated as sacrosanct.*

*Any such venture would at once impact on our light into the kitchen and our views from all three levels of our property, yet we have not heard a word about whatever is going on.*

*Can you please throw some light on this matter as a matter of urgency.*

*Regards*

Note the deliberate use of the word "sacrosanct" as a negotiating ploy. The principle might have been bust now but the writer was still drawing on the history of the last thirty years in the hope that the secretary might see the point having fulfilled his own objectives! This line of argument was clearly likely to assume some significance with members as there had obviously been a strong following for it prior to the introduction of the new rules which most had had little or no time to contemplate.

## The response

*Hi*

*Thanks for your message. I'm in Scotland this week but, as far as I am aware, no formal approach has been made to directors or myself about any proposed development at No 123*

*Should such an approach be made I will of course let you and other shareholders know at the earliest opportunity.*

*With kind regards*

*(Secretary)*

What did that suggest!?

First of all, that I had indeed struck the first blow.

Secondly the secretary had copied the message to each of the directors other than Paul himself. Now I was in a position by merely responding to this letter I could by copy draw them into any comments I would now make! This would be seen as a quite natural action which would potentially be much to my advantage! Better than jumping in too soon and circulating all and sundry direct in a state of panic. As a technique such opportunities should not be disregarded!

My response:

*Thank you,.*

*I have seen various folk, including our local builder measuring up. comparing bricks etc. together with what I deduce to be a surveyor taking measurements and so on.*

*Do enjoy your trip to Scotland*

*Regards*

(A good time to extend pleasantries which should be noted!)

This was soon followed by the next correspondence:

*Hi,*

*Further to our recent email correspondence, on my return from Scotland this morning, I found a letter from the council informing me (as a resident) that a planning application has been submitted for a single-story extension to (address) (Reference number). I think it likely that, as a near neighbour, you will have received the same information letter. In addition, there was a letter from the Architect, addressed to myself as secretary of the management company, formally informing us of this application and including plans etc. I have forwarded this correspondence to the directors in the first instance and will await their response and comments.*

*I hope this is helpful.*

*With kind regards*

*(Secretary)*

Now the fight was on two fronts. Firstly the Planning Department and then the Management Company. Since planning applications take some time as a rule I had bought myself time to attempt by all means to win my argument with the company.

The builder had set up a pyramid of bricks for the benefit of a visiting planning officer that clearly indicated which would be used in the construction.

They were of sufficiently different size, colour and style that the author drew attention to this matter both to planning and the company. So far as planning were concerned this was reputed to be inconsequential since bricks can always be manufactured, they said, to any specification. Next the surveyor was seen photographing the pyramid the builder had set up at close range, and not the wall of bricks that the extension was supposed to match. It was obvious that he intended to present this photograph to planning to justify the bricks they intended to use, this being a complete misrepresentation of the actual bricks. The author again made much of this to both the company and to planning. Both again were alerted to the possible precedent approval of the application would set in motion, not to mention the gradual erosion of the character of the courtyard. Beyond that Paul's house itself would be disfigured by the proposed development, and be an ugly stain on the courtyard. Finally it was suggested that there was more than one method by which the need for a downstairs toilet and shower could be accommodated. It was urged that in the interest of all parties these be properly considered. All meticulously set out in written form as in such a case nothing else would be appropriate.

It all fell on deaf ears, but I had given it my best.

Whilst the verdict of the Planning department was still awaited the writer had next to turn his attention to winning over the officers and members of the management company. Rushing into correspondence with all other general members would be premature and detract from the goodwill the writer would require. Furthermore, the only property that would be directly affected by the proposal would be that of the writer himself, so he could expect nothing but apathy from the remainder. So corresponding with the shareholders had to be put on hold until more facts were ascertained and the writer had something more powerful to say. It was time to respond to the secretary again now the planning department application was in progress.

A window of opportunity was open that, in acknowledging the secretary's message, the writer could now advance some lines of argument designed especially to influence the independent directors to whom the message would also be circulated.

The message read as follows:

*Hi Secretary*

*Thank you.*

*I had received the planning letter on Saturday but decided not to intrude again into your holiday. As the result would seriously affect our treasured views of the common land, which in the past has always been held as sacrosanct, my intention will inevitably be to fight against the proposal. And not least because (Paul) has had the gumption to go to all the expense of setting the building up and applying for planning permission without as much as a prior word to the company. This shows a bold assumption that he will get his own way, no doubt because most folk will be apathetic to my situation as long as it doesn't affect their own.*

*In days gone by it was always understood that our common land afforded each property rather wonderful views from each location, and that once a precedent was created others would think of inventive ways to follow suit to their own advantage. At that time (Tony) resolutely refused to budge one iota over the principle. That way nobody would be put under extreme anxiety and nobody would ask because they knew what the response would be.*

*Now any such development in any corner of the court would impact one way or another on the views, the right of way, or the privacy of others. And we will all be sitting anxiously waiting for somebody to come up with the next inventive idea that will ruin the day for one or other of us. I do hope this will be stopped now at source and the directors will see the common sense of blocking this development.*

*Moreover, whilst the Articles are not specific on the point, I have always believed that since we all own the common land jointly no one party should be allowed to do anything to infringe upon these rights without the unanimous agreement of all. That is to say that any vote taken based upon a mere majority is not nearly sufficiently protective of the common land, and at once impinges upon the understood right of each member to fully enjoy the courtyard unimpeded.*

*As to the actual proposal, from what I have gleamed my views from the lounge we use constantly at the rear will be significantly restricted, as would be the case actually on all three floors and the kitchen would lose its light just where (my wife) works at the sink. I am extremely disturbed and anxious about this suggestion having paid good money for our property, influenced in particular by its location and the unique views of the courtyard itself.*

*Thank you for keeping me updated.*

It pays usually to be assertive and provide the solution rather than just ask the question. Note also that I argue the kitchen would "lose its light", being expressed as an absolute and not by degree (as in "a significant amount" of.) It reads as though the kitchen will be as good as plunged into darkness, whereas the softer approach of saying the light "would be reduced" as another example is far less effective. The stronger poetic license used will be fixed in the minds of the addressees who are more likely to take it at face value, and be duly impressed, than turn up to make an objective assessment with a light meter! The right terminology has a lasting impact, especially when it is read back on review by interested parties subsequently. If it is taken as read you are already on a winning streak!

I continued to argue the line that the courtyard should be regarded as "sacrosanct" but the genii was out of the bag now and this line of argument would only do me any good so long as any of the directors had lingering doubts over the new rules the secretary had in effect imposed on us all.

Needless to say, his response came back based on a forensic review of the legal situation (which really missed the point) as follows:

*Hi*

*Thank you for your email message and my apologies for not replying more fully until now.*

*As mentioned in my email of…… I passed on your comments and concerns to the three directors (i.e., those not directly involved in the application) for consideration.*

*It may be helpful to remind you that, as was agreed at the 20... AGM, there is a defined process by which requests for any change within the court, made by any shareholder, should be considered. This was specifically to ensure that any request should be viewed objectively, with directors taking account of various aspects of the impact or effects of the proposed change on other shareholders. I attach a copy of this agreement for your information.*

*Should there be a disagreement, the process as outlined in the guidelines, would be for the matter initially to be discussed by shareholders at either an EGM or the AGM. In the current situation we hope to be able to hold the delayed AGM in the near future so that, if necessary, this can be discussed then, along with other business.*

*You will note incidentally, that the guidelines specifically highlight the fact that no precedent will be established by any individual agreement, and that any application for change will be considered on its own merits.*

*This process is of course quite separate to the formal planning application process through the local Council Planning Department.*

*I anticipate that, once they have discussed the matter fully, the directors will be in touch to give you feedback as soon as possible, and well ahead of any General Meeting. I hope this is helpful.*

*With kind regards*

*(Secretary)*


So now he had his own style rules, (critical to turning around his own earlier case) and he was now defending them at all costs! The word "sacrosanct" had been ceremoniously deleted from his vocabulary!

As to his contention that the rules were protective because they meant any applications would have to be viewed "objectively" one wonders how that would be when it would fall to the subjective opinions of the management as to how they should be interpreted! And to say that it was provided that no single approved application would be permitted to "create a precedent" was fresh when it was his own application the year before that had changed the path of history over the previous thirty years! But that offered me another hostage to fort I could take up and build upon!

Each communication was made with the intention of prompting some kind of response. It was hoped that such responses would give more grounds to argue or present the case, perhaps reveal some weakness or other conceded by the Secretary and his director cliche. It was all rather cat and mouse to coin a phrase.

Response:

*Hi (Secretary)*

*Thank you for taking the trouble to guide me on the action you have taken, and for providing me with a copy of the rules adopted at the 2019 meeting from which we were unavoidably absent. I much preferred the previous approach which I understand had stood for some thirty years etc. etc.*

*The directors took responsibility for protecting the long-term interests of the courtyard and all the shareholders with an interest therein. Once such matters are put up to the shareholders for a general vote, democratic as this is in the right circumstances, a mixture of vested interests, apathy and detachment enters the matter such that any decision taken is likely to be distorted or short term orientated and potentially dangerously impacting on procedures for a long time into the future. Once a precedent is created it is very difficult to find a road back to the status quo.*

*Having studied the 20... rules in detail it is very clear to me, (and should be to the directors), that an undesirable precedent would be introduced were (Paul's) application to be accepted. So it ought to be a shut and closed case right there as it would undoubtedly affect our property, but I am unclear as to how it is proposed the board intend to proceed from this point on. For example, will it be the case that the directors will protect long term mutual interests outside the meeting as before. If the directors decide against the proposal, will they still take it to a general vote in which case their judgement will most likely be disregarded by apathy of those not affected, or otherwise. Will the directors be making a recommendation and then leave it to chance what happens, or just how is it envisaged this will be determined!?*

*As to (Paul's) application it would present us with an even larger area of brickwork just feet away than already exists. It would make the sink area of the kitchen dark and the outlook more foreboding. Because of the angles involved and the strategic placing of the proposal it would ruin our view of that side of the courtyard, the features in it, and the amenity to that side from all three floors, etc. etc.*

*I have always taken the view that if you invest in a property sharing communal facilities in such a special spot within a conservation area you should make your mind up if it is what you really require before going ahead with the purchase. The alternative of invading communal space and putting others out of joint is simply not tenable, fair or reasonable.*

*We spend most of our time in the lounge at the rear facing Edward's wall of brickwork, etc. etc. The development would take this away to the one side and make the large scale of brickwork facing us all the more daunting.*

*The proposal does not merely impact upon us, but would give his property an unwieldy, unnatural shape with the end section protruding out of proportion to the remainder. He already has a bathroom, and if he requires another facility, I am sure he can find an alternative means of achieving this. If voted in, and I'm sorry on (Paul's) behalf to say this, it would clearly cement the precedent that nobody's view of the courtyard or its many features or general amenity matters any more. If this is voted in it would surely open the floodgates to owners with inventive minds and nobody will be safe ever again and the courtyard would suffer. His property would evolve in an unnatural and disproportionate shape thus spoiling the general look of the courtyard. Even the bricks on display are of a different size, hue and colour, so that the whole area of brickwork would not be consistent along its length.*

*It would be a tragedy if this proposal were permitted against the rules set out you have already provided me with, not only for ourselves but for all that follow. If the currently adopted rules are to mean anything then please do not permit this to happen.*

*Best regards*

I regret to say that I have fallen into the trap here in a serious way of being somewhat verbose, something I have advised my readers against throughout this chapter! My only defence is that there were a lot of points to make! But the fight was really warming up now! So what might this communication have had in mind when it was written?

1. It would keep the "sanctity" line of argument in the picture.
2. It would flatter (Tony) and hopefully win his vote as he had always been an advocate for no change.
3. It would score all of the arguments at the writer's disposal in one last desperate attempt.
4. It would make the point that we were absent when the new rules were adopted.
5. It was an attempt to keep the vote outside the general meeting. If the author could not win the officers over outside the meeting, there would be no chance he could do so within.
6. If the issue went to a general vote of all shareholders, then the vested interests would win set against the certain apathy of the remainder.
7. It would omen badly for the future.
8. It was a heaven-sent opportunity to actually quote the new rules to the writer's advantage. Whilst it might be argued that his points were weak, nevertheless by making the right assertions strongly they would hopefully stick!
9. It would throw the cat amongst the pigeons should the directors' approach be potentially overridden by the shareholders.
10. It argued our case as strongly as possible.

If the recipients of this communication conceded that aspects of the application would be ultra vires the new rules then how could they possibly allow it through!? Little by little I was beginning to make some ground, and I was still in there fighting from my corner!

The next response,
*Hi*

*Thanks for your further message reiterating the concerns you have regarding the Application by (Paul) to extend his property in order to provide a downstairs toilet and shower at ...*

*The directors are considering this request, using the agreed guidelines as a guide in making their decision and recommendation, and will feed back to you in the very near future. I will leave that to them but thought I should respond to the important points you raise about procedure and understandings.*

*The previous approach you preferred to was in fact very weak in substance. There was, and remains, no mention at all in any of the legal documentation associated with the (Articles of Association/Deed of Covenant etc.) that the communal land is sacrosanct or in any way protected. The 'understanding' was based entirely on a verbal assurance and, as such, could be challenged at any time, with no documentation available to guide directors or shareholders in making an objective response. Neither would this 'verbal assurance' be available or evident to a prospective purchaser of a property within the courtyard.*

*In 20... this was discussed and the guidelines now in place were drawn up and agreed. While it might have been possible, and probably in your view desirable, to simply ban any change or development in xyz court, this was rejected because there was an acceptance that people's situation and needs change over time and that, if a proposed change was able to satisfy the points made in the guidelines, it would be unreasonable to refuse approval. In the current instance, without pre-judging the decision of directors, the guidelines have provided you with a much stronger case as your own concerns will have to be addressed using the headings provided.*

*One key point to note is that the guidelines ensure an Objective approach is taken, rather than a Subjective one in which personal friendships or loyalties could influence judgements. All the points you have made in your two emails are noted and can now be considered carefully and objectively and I anticipate the directors will give you feedback in the very near future.*

*Thank you again for your message.*

*With best wishes*

*(Secretary)*

At last, a stunning admission that the writer had "strong arguments" The best way forward now would be to respond urgently thus underscoring this admission before any negative comments landed on his desk. It would not have been made without reference to the directors, and now he would emphasise the point they could not overlook what they had already conceded!

The fact that the secretary had, as he said, "stepped aside" from any decision of the directors would also serve as a clever sidestep away from any liability on his part to stand by Paul. Any quid pro quo understanding with Paul would thus be blunted.

Of course, the secretary was technically right about the issue of "sanctity of the courtyard" if you wanted to apply forensic legal considerations, but the adopted approach had stood very well to everybody's satisfaction for thirty years so the author still felt he was missing the point – not that he would ever be willing to conceded this having himself been the architect for change.

But I wasn't quite done yet!
I penned the following:

Hi (Secretary)

*Thank you for your helpful comments.*

*I do wholeheartedly concede there may always be circumstances wherein everybody would accept a given request was reasonable, and could not be resisted, so anything written into the rules themselves adjudging all common land to be sacrosanct would as you say be a mistake. For such cases my personal preference would be for a stipulated unanimous or, say two thirds approval requirement which obviates any dispute as to whether it has been judged objectively or not. Usually with common land it is always in a confined space when one person's gain is inevitably another's loss, and this is where in my experience it has without exception actually been treated as sacrosanct. But I'm sure we could go on debating this ad infinitum!*

*Suffice to say we do have a well-reasoned set of rules arising out of the 20... meeting so I do hope, should it be determined by the directors (as I would feel appropriate) that (Paul's) request offends these rules, it will not be permitted to proceed into a general vote which could end up with unintended consequences and create conflicting precedents directly opposed to the rules.*

*I take much heart in your acknowledgement that we do have serious arguments on our side and look forward to hearing from the directors as you have indicated, most desirably before the planning department makes its ruling. Were this to be successful in its own right ahead of our deliberations then I'm sure it would be offered up as a line of argument, which no doubt we would all contemplate given the same situation.*

*Thank you for your kind attention to this matter.*

Time to be conciliatory! So the debate on the sanctity of the courtyard was concluded with my having the final say! Always best to agree to disagree when possible, especially at a rather critical stage of the negotiations!

Now the author was evermore quoting the new rules himself in support of his own case. If your counterpart concedes something as important as admitting you have strong arguments then consolidate your position still further by quoting this back to them. And not least because those copies of the correspondence circulated to the other parties will emphasise the point to them also, and make it all the harder for them to find against you!

The point about unintended consequences was a serious point, firstly designed to make them think, and secondly in another effort to encourage the directors to come to a conclusion without permitting the matter to go to a general vote. This also emphasised the need to communicate their decision sooner than later – as was the point about the near impending result of the planning department. If external planning permission were to be granted before they had communicated a decision then it would certainly do much to support Paul's case.

And finally the much-awaited letter arrived on the author's doorstep

*Good morning,*

*I am writing to inform you that the directors have arrived at a unanimous decision to recommend to the shareholders that the planned extension at No 2… be turned down on the grounds that it does not satisfy the first two criteria of the guidelines laid down in 20…*

*I do hope that the directors decision goes some way to alleviating your concerns.*

*All the best*

*(Chairman)*

Eureka!

It was now near enough certain, given the numbers, that the request would fail. To which the following response was penned to cover all eventualities.

*Hi (Chairman)*

*Thank you so much. That really is a great relief.*

*Does that mean however that it will still be put to a vote!?*

*You will be aware from my comments on the issue that I am deeply concerned that, should any general vote find in favour of the proposal then not only would I be the loser after all, but we would end up with the hideous position that something would be left to stand even though it directly offended the rules! What then would this mean for the future if anybody else wanted to go against the rules!?*

*You will already be aware that I am hoping to be in a position to take my wife away for a few weeks much needed recuperation after she has been ill since January now, so the date of any meeting would be critical to me should it be necessary for us to attend.*

*Best regards*

*John*

It seemed as though the odds were heavily stacked against the writer at the outset, but by a series of small gains little by little the case was turned around and the proposed intrusion finally averted. The author's adversaries were clearly not without keen negotiating experience in their own right, and had already proved to be belligerent towards members until now so it was a well fought result.

Negotiations in written form such as the foregoing abound in many walks of life. It may be in pursuit of compensation claims, job applications, legal defences, service complaints and many more besides. Always marshal your key points into a list before setting about framing them into your correspondence. Always assert your key strengths as you see them even if that is a subjective judgement. Watch for admissions and concessions in the responses you receive, and underscore them by commencing your communications by acknowledging what the other party has said in your favour. Jump on any "hostages to fort" and make the best of them!

Notice particularly that these entire negotiations from start to finish were all conducted in the written form with no direct words being exchanged. There was absolutely no verbal contact whatever on the matter.

Perhaps in hindsight this was a mistake!

Even though all the arguments were made to Planning, and they were informed ahead of their verdict that the management company had turned down the application, they found in favour as it was always assumed they would. Moreover they made little of the light problem, stating it was more than adequate as provided by other windows in the kitchen.

Needless to say Paul made much of this. He was also seen limping badly around the premises in what appeared for all the world to emphasise the difficulty he was experiencing in climbing his stairs to his facilities. Moreover he withdrew from all communication with members around the courtyard, and was clearly milking all the sympathy he could get. Concerned neighbours knocked on his door to enquire if he was alright, and he pleaded he just "didn't feel like coming out at present!" And in his newfound capacity of Director he did what the author would have no doubt done himself. He asked his colleague directors for the issue to be taken to an extraordinary meeting to be determined by all the shareholders at large. The cliche hardened behind him using the unfortunate Planning comments in regard to lighting as fodder backing their change of position in spite of the fact they used different rules, for example excluding the question of views from their deliberations altogether. Having actually advised the author that they were against the application, they were now backing a full vote in general meeting, no doubt having little alternative. As a long-established resident of the courtyard Paul went about encouraging his friends to give him their vote, over-egging his so-called weak knee to establish his case.

The Secretary circulated voting papers to all members ahead of the meeting giving them the opportunity to vote before they had even heard the matter debated in person. That little ruse placed members in a position to vote on the basis of old friendships even without having debated the matter in general meeting even for a minute! The strength of the cliche, the old pals act, skulduggery and the acting ability of Paul in regard to his weak knee all finally won the day for him.

After all that work and expectation the author had for once lost a negotiation he had staked so much upon. Paul's knee made a miraculous recovery and he was last seen taking his strong dog around the local park at a fair old pace, no hint of his so-called injury on view. The extension went up, but by then massive trees in the neighbours grounds had been cleared. Whilst some of the courtyard was lost to view from the rear rooms the compensating views opened up by the tree felling operation more than compensated.

So what were the final lessons to be learned. Of course never get complacent. The temporary victory when the directors confirmed their position might have given an opportunity to consolidate the position had the author ignored his own advice and indulged in vocal discussions with each and every one of them immediately afterwards.    Just to create a rapport and cement his hard won position.    So this constitutes a warning against complacency and says that even apparently clearcut victories still have to be consolidated with further action. The author had to admit to himself that he should immediately have got around to the directors on foot playing the 'old boys' approach whilst he was winning. Failure to do so meant he had not sufficiently cemented his gains. So above all that was where he went wrong at the last hurdle, but not altogether surprisingly so as they were a rather unpleasant bunch of individuals!

It also highlights the power in local communities of cliches and of the old pals act. The author found this in the apartment run by the so called "residents committee" which resisted the purchase by members of the freeholds discussed earlier. But that issue ended on a happier note.

The principles set out above are clearly the right ones to follow, and were it not for the skulduggery that followed they had had the desired effect. But approaches can always be improved upon and more direct contact in the above case might have been the missing ingredient. But the final lesson to be learned is that you can't necessarily win them all. If you fail then cut your losses, swallow your pride and carry on regardless!

**Key Tactics Summary**

Marshal your key points before composing your communication.

Negotiating in the written form has strong arguments in its favor

A well written letter is an enormous aid and can of itself determine the outcome.

You can set traps in the written form which are easily missed, disregarded, overlooked or forgotten in vocal negotiations.

A single well chosen word can be hugely effective.

Don't be too verbose (with apologies from the author for breaking his own rule!)

Hold your own when it matters but back off when this has served its purpose.

Be conciliatory and exchange normal pleasantries to keep the hat on any rising animosities.

Many negotiations only can be resolved through the written media and that alone.

Always look to gain from your experiences over time.

Take failures graciously and remember you can't win them all!

# Chapter 30
# The Wooden Spoon

The entire planning system is rife with potential for negotiation. You could say it is all about negotiating the best outcome against a backcloth of local rules wherein mistakes and miscarriages of justice do arise. Planning departments operate in an atmosphere when procedure is almost as important as the substance of a case.

However my runner up for the wooden spoon is not any planning department but the very well-known and much respected Everest Windows company.

When we bought our grade two listed property in a Georgian market town we took the opportunity to pay that small fee to have the local conservation manager come around for an informal review prior to submitting any planning applications. We always felt this was an excellent negotiating ploy in itself since he was so pleased he had been called upon to offer his professional advice he fell over backwards telling us in effect what we could get away with. We had plenty to discuss, part of which concerned a single window which needed replacement due to a privacy issue with neighbours. Establish that that could be double glazed and the principle could be extended hopefully to the entire property. In discussing the matter I quietly used the almost forbidden phrase "double glazed." I made so little of this in fact, knowing I was on shaky ground, that no reference to it appeared in the notes to the meeting he subsequently produced. At the next meeting I showed him an excellent mock-up of a double glazed window frame which had been engineered by a specialist company in wood. A puzzled look crossed his face and he reached for his notes to see what he had said about the proposition. Of course there was nothing but I was in a position of pointing out to him exactly where we stood when I raised the subject, and I could see he was much impressed with the product.

In the meantime Everest declined to quote or negotiate at all since they did not want to waste good money in doing so when they "knew any such application would fail."

However it succeeded and the windows for the entire house were changed impacting enormously on both their effectiveness for warmth and their appearance. They also eliminated the noise of folk exiting the local pubs at night. A new precedent had been set for the entire conservation area, and household after household flocked to buy the same product in the certain knowledge that planning would now be granted.

Everest lost out! The Everest representative did call around again subsequently with a sheepish look on his face to enquire further into the matter, perhaps hoping to find we had proceeded against the law. We showed him the planning consent, and he left a very disappointed and embarrassed individual.

The winner of the wooden spoon concerns just two or three large windows also in a conservation area, but this time not in a listed property. One window in particular concerned planning. They argued it could be seen by passing public, and would spoil the ethos of the area even though it was back some distance from the road. Between the pavement and the property was a small garden area in which grew some foliage which we commonly refer to as palms but which are in fact another variety. There were gaps in this greenery through which it would be true to say you could clearly see the main window, but if you took a photograph directed more towards the thickest part of the growth then the window was barely visible. And it was just such a photograph I submitted, tongue in cheek, with my application. But despite this attempt the application failed merely on the principle that the council were hard set against PVC windows this time, so we decided to go on to appeal the decision.

The appeal hearing gave me just five minutes to present my carefully prepared case, but prior to that a no nonsense council member who abhorred the local attitude against pvc windows was invited to express her views. To say the least she was very sharp.

Astonishingly, instead of taking his own damaging photograph the objecting planning officer had used my photo to present his case. He even went to the trouble of setting up an overhead projector so you could see it in full glory on a large screen.

The councillor with the delightful name of Mrs Boosey responded to his opening statement.

*"Could you just show me on the projector screen where the offending window is please?"*

The minutes passed whilst the flustered officer attempted to point his rod at the precise area of the window, but failed. In the end he merely claimed.

*"It's around there I think!"*
*"I rest my case"*
said Mrs Boosey, and sat herself down again with a sigh.

My much prepared statement was already more or less redundant, and the planning objection was at once overturned. The panning officer had been led, through carelessness or laziness, down the path of using my photograph to support his case. He had shot himself in the foot, or to coin a phrase first introduced in the chapter on haggling, he had "done a Joseph!" This time around Planning got the wooden spoon!

# Chapter 31
# Conclusion

We have seen that negotiation is all pervasive in all walks of life. It can start in a strictly orthodox way, as a chat in the loo, or even a glance. Preparation is always the best road to success. Determining in advance what you seek to achieve is fundamental. If you have the right tools, native wit, personality, patience and determination you will be well equipped to obtain the maximum outcome. You are selling your personality as much as anything, inspiring faith and trust in your ability to carry out what you have undertaken. You should expect negotiations to be carried out in a cordial spirit and seek to achieve this. Be affable yet prepared to meet like with like if the negotiations are hostile. Know human nature and know how to recognise what is going on by reading the signals. Don't be taken for a fool, but learn how to handle failures. Failures better prepare you to deal with similar situations in the future, so move on and learn from the experience. Don't put backs up to no purpose. It achieves nothing in the long term! Be humble and make friends, not enemies! Spot nepotism when you encounter it as this will heavily influence the approach you take. Beware idle flattery, and don't win "too well." See enemies coming, read petty jealousies, avoid those adopted by power driven individuals, and don't be intimidated.

Anticipating what your opposing number most values or you might offer him will assist you handsomely. No negotiation will ever be successful unless both parties go away satisfied they have procured the best deal possible in the circumstances. So you have to reach out to the other's point of view, seek out what it is he values and ask yourself what it is you might offer him to break through any deadlock. If you are facing an unwelcome and unavoidable situation you have all the more need to fight with your back against the wall, employing every tool at your disposal. Sometimes you have to become a "political animal." What is good in politics can be employed in business, even in our private lives.

Above all, in your anxiety to reach a deal never give away trade secrets or confidential information which can do you harm!

Nothing has ever given me greater pleasure than making a "profit" out of a "disaster" to the point that each time something potentially disastrous confronts me, other than of a personal nature, I naturally look for the profit in it! Speed is usually of the essence so know your priorities, and don't spoil the entire approach for the want of haggling over some insignificant detail! Check lists are a very useful tool, especially in negotiations that repeat themselves over time. As an example, in a company occupied with takeovers I once drew up a check list covering all the many areas that fall for consideration each time a company is taken over. It served as a useful point of reference if only for progress control. So be methodical always and not haphazard.

High cost complex issues are being negotiated at Government level today, some of which have been so for a number of years. Such negotiations are a world apart from the simpler ones most of us encounter, but simple as they may be it takes extra effort to maximise the outcome. Larger contracts may of course take months and years before they come to fruition.

There is so much in the subject it can be baffling to those starting out, but of immeasurable value to your careers as you gain experience. Enjoy the task. Negotiations are challenging but they bring results, and they should be fun and fulfilling as opposed to being regarded as a chore. I would guarantee that if the mindset is negative then the result will not have been optimised. In a bland choice between two alternatives only one will come out the winner so accept that with good grace. Don't expect to win every time. Look for the win-win outcome but if there is no such beast available then satisfy yourself you have given your best effort. Accept the outcome in good faith and move on. Don't mope as it will only distract from other important matters of the day and won't change the outcome.

You could say I owe everything I have to negotiation. It has always been the successful outcome of negotiations that has drawn attention to my abilities. For myself personally it has been like a rich vein running through my entire life. If you are fortunate enough to pull off a most improbable negotiation, as for example like that in my chapter on banking, then your superiors will naturally look to you the next time such a proposition is in the offing. Your position can only be enhanced or substantiated. It has not only been the highlight of my career but was the main contributing factor enabling me to retire early to pursue other interests.

My readers may have different ambitions of course, but it has given me both fun and satisfaction at home and around the world. I hope there will be something for everybody in these pages and they will both stimulate you and complement your knowledge of this vast subject. May the reading of this work do nothing but bring you success. The sky is the limit. You may reach the heights of negotiating on the international stage, introduce far reaching political and fiscal reforms, join or leave trading blocks, rise to the Cabinet or higher, or pull off world breaking deals in all walks of life. Or you may find satisfaction knowing that in whatever role you are occupied, and in private life, your negotiating skills have played their part to your satisfaction. Wherever you are always view negotiation as an opportunity, and never as a necessary evil or a drudge. It can and should be a highly profitable occupation. May it bring you a rich vein of enjoyment! So do have fun along the way and enjoy the success I wish all my readers!

*The author feigning the signing of a peace Treaty between the United States and North Korea, taken in the office bridging the 38th parallel. Half of this office protrudes into South Korea and was established specifically as a venue to commence negotiations which could one day make a major contribution to world peace. This area is acknowledged by many to be the most dangerous location in the world. Rather astonishingly it was taken by the Camp Commandant himself, one of the very top military officers in North Korea.*